EARTH STORIES

EARTH STORIES

· · · · ·

*Signs of God's
Love and Mystery*

———

JOHN R. AURELIO

CONTINUUM • NEW YORK

1997

The Continuum Publishing Company
370 Lexington Avenue, New York, NY 10017

Copyright © 1997 by John R. Aurelio

Printed in the United States of America

Library of Congress Cataloging-in-Publication Data

Aurelio, John.
    Earth stories : signs of God's love and mystery / John R. Aurelio.
        p.   cm.
    ISBN 0-8264-0949-0 (hc : alk. paper)
    1. Nature—Religious aspects—Christianity—Fiction.
 2. Inspiration—Religious aspects—Christianity—Fiction.
 I. Title.
PS3551.U76E28   1997
813'. 54—dc21   96-48455
                                                                          CIP

To Nature . . .

God's first Book of Revelation

———

CONTENTS

CONTENTS

WAVE

*O*nce upon a time, deep below the vast ocean floor, the earth felt an itch (or something) and twitched. The tremor stirred the deep waters and caused the ocean to experience a slight shudder. When the shudder rose to the surface like a goose bump, Wave was born.

"Wow!"

That's the first thing he said as he looked out at the world surrounding him. Stretching from one end of the horizon to the other like an enormous mantle was a brilliant blue sky. "I like that," Wave thought. "I like blue." Why, he was so impressed with the color blue that he decided to keep it to himself and make it a part of him.

Next, he noticed some fluffy white clouds floating into view. "Aren't they beautiful," he sighed. "High and white and so many interesting shapes." As each one passed overhead, it made a deep impression on him and continued on.

As more clouds rolled by, Wave tried to hold on to them all, but he didn't have enough room in him so he had to let some of them go. For the first time in his new life he felt sadness. "I guess some things have to go to make room for other things." Life was quickly forcing its lessons upon him.

Then a voice like a strong whisper swept over him. "Move along," it said. "You mustn't dally. We have places to go and things to do, and you're holding up everybody else. Move along."

Wave looked around but didn't see anything. "Who spoke just now?" he asked.

"I did," the voice replied.

"Who are you?"

"I am the wind."

Wave looked around expecting to see someone or something. "Where are you? I don't see you."

Now, winds not only are serious about their work, they also are very pushy and haven't much time to hang around and shoot the breeze. They have to fill the sails of sailing ships, spin the wheels of busy windmills, shake the fruit from overburdened trees, carry seeds around the earth, cool off people hot from the sun, and do a lot of other important things. All this Wave would have known if any of these things had crossed his path, but he was young and everything was still very new to him.

"You can't see me," the wind said, "but, you can feel me. I'm the one who has been pushing you along all this time."

To tell the truth, Wave didn't even know that he was being pushed. He just thought that waves move because he couldn't imagine one that didn't. What he didn't know was that he was being pushed.

"Where are you pushing me?"

"You'll see. You'll see," the wind said and repeated. "It's time to move on. I mustn't lose myself in idle chatter when there's so much work to be done. The more I talk the weaker I become and the less work I'll be able to do. 'Move on' is all I can say or should say. Move on. Move on." He kept repeating this until his voice faded away.

Well, Wave did as he was urged and continued on. The blue sky and white clouds continued to fill his thoughts when something fell from out of nowhere right on top of him.

"Ooof!" Wave grunted.

"Splash!" the pelican said.

"What's that?" Wave asked.

"The expression is 'splash.' When something hits you you're supposed to say 'splash.' You must be new at this."

"Why do you say that?"

"Listen kid. I've done this over a thousand times and it's always the same—'splash!' Always 'splash, splash, splash.' Big Waves, little waves—makes no difference. 'Ooof' goes with 'poof' and that's wind talk. You must have been talking to that blowhard. Wave talk is 'splash,' so you might as well get it right from the start."

"I'll try to remember," Wave said, hoping he wouldn't forget the way he was already forgetting the clouds that had passed out of sight. "I won't forget if I hold on to him," he thought, but the pelican would have none of it. He flapped his wings and wiggled his feet. Wave discovered for the first time that he was ticklish. When he squirmed, the bird broke free.

"We do it every time," he cackled back at him. "If we didn't there would be none of us left to tell the tale. You've still got a lot of growing to do, my young friend." Having said that the pelican began to fly off.

"Splash!" Wave yelled.

The pelican turned back. "You've got it all wrong, kid. You only say 'splash' when someone drops in on you."

"What do you say when they leave?"

"Nothing. Just wave."

The pelican flew off and Wave waved good-bye.

Shortly afterwards Wave felt something tickling him again. He looked around but the sky was clear of birds. "What could be causing this?" he wondered. Once again, he felt the tickling sensation. He felt like rippling, like yelling, "Splash, splash, splash," and sending little drops of hilarity into the breeze. He might have laughed, "Heh, heh, heh," if he had known about laughter, but after his encounter with the pelican he wasn't sure if splash weren't the only way waves are supposed to react.

He looked around some more, but no one was dropping in on him that he could see. At least not outside. But, there was definitely something moving around inside of him. It was a fish. The fish paused for a second, giving Wave a moment of relief. Then, it wiggled its tail and moved its fins again, only very fast. Not knowing how to giggle, Wave tried to hold it in. As he did he got bigger and bigger like someone holding his breath. He thought he was going to burst when he heard the fish say, "Thank you. Now I can see better what's up ahead."

The comment caught Wave unawares, and thinking about it eased his tension. "What is that supposed to mean?" he asked.

The fish stopped what he was about to do. "You were a little too small for me to see very far ahead," he answered.

"So you tickled me?"

"So I tickled you."

"Why?"

"To get a rise out of you?"

"What does that mean?"

"Precisely what I said," the fish replied as if surprised that Wave hadn't learned this by now. "When we fish tickle you with our fins and gills, you swell up with laughter. However, since waves can't laugh, you just keep getting bigger. The bigger you get, the farther ahead we can see from inside of you."

"I was just about ready to explode," Wave said.

"I knew that," the fish replied. "I was just about to fly free and let you calm down again when you stopped me by talking to me."

Once again, Wave was confused. "Are you a bird?"

"No. I'm a fish."

"Do fish fly like birds?"

"Flying fish like me do. That's why we want to see what's

ahead before we break out of the water. Otherwise we might fly into something like a boat or a shoal and hurt ourselves."

The world about him was not only wonderful, Wave thought, but strange and confusing. There was so much to learn and remember. Would he remember all these things as he grew up?

When the fish tickled him again he let himself swell up until she broke free. She soared into the air in magnificent flight; and even though it didn't last very long, it was a very impressive flight nonetheless. "Perhaps we'll meet up again," Wave thought.

Many more things were to fill up Wave's first day. There were ships that moved back and forth across the ocean, dolphins and whales that leaped and frolicked, planes flying overhead like birds and fish, and occasional flotsam and jetsam. He found these unusual things especially diverting.

As evening drew on Wave was approaching some even more memorable experiences. Unaccountably, he was beginning to move much faster than before even though the wind was not pushing him any harder. Some new force was drawing him forward, making him bigger and stronger.

"It's me," the moon said smiling down at him.

"How are you doing this to me?" Wave asked.

"Because I am irresistibly attractive, I affect everything on the earth," she answered.

Indeed, Wave found himself so attracted to the moon that if he could have, he would have reached all the way up to touch her. Not being able to didn't stop him from trying.

"You are truly irresistible," he called out to her.

"I know," she replied. "It's my nature."

"Watch out how you brag, hag!" chided the setting sun.

"Don't listen to him," she said coolly. "He's just jealous because he's too far away to influence you. Watch out for him, though. He's got a hot temper. Stay cool and he can't hurt you. Me? I bring out the best in you."

"Listen to her, will you? Why, without me she's nothing," the sun retaliated. "She's nothing but a reflection of me . . . and a poor one at that."

"What did I tell you?" the moon whispered to Wave. "See how quickly he flares up. If you ask me it's all show. He's nothing but a big showoff."

"And you're nothing but a fickle face," the sun shot back. "Don't trust her, son. She's always changing her face. When you see her smile, you never know if it's you that she's snickering at."

"Don't listen to him. He's just trying to warm up to you. Let him and he's sure to burn you up."

"Not so. What I do is make you warm and comfortable so that life can abound in and around you. With all her coolness, can she do that?"

"I can make him swell with pride."

"And then bring him crashing down."

Wave stopped the bickering by saying, "I like you both." With that, the sun started sinking into the ocean and the moon began moving off into the distance. Wave felt a chill. He sensed that everything was rapidly approaching an end.

There were strange sounds up ahead. He stretched as high as he could, this time so that he could see farther. He saw huge waves like himself crashing into the shore. It looked exciting. There were people laughing and playing in the foam. "Isn't that wonderful," he thought. So this was where it was all heading. It seemed like fun.

At that moment someone pointed to him and shouted to the others, "There's a good one!" They all came swimming out to him, some on surf boards or tubes or inflatable rafts. "We're going to love this one."

Wave could barely hear above the growing din. But, when

he heard the word *love,* a whole new sensation came over him. It made him feel warm and good . . . even better than the sun did. Love made him feel warm in a different way. People made him feel this way. Maybe it was because their bodies were warm as they moved into him. The fish were all cool. So, too, were his recollections of the clouds, the planes, and the boats. True, the sun was warm, but it warmed him from the outside. People were warming him from inside and it felt wonderful. He was so excited that he knew he was going to yell out one really big, SPLASH! when he and all of them went tumbling happily into the shore.

Suddenly, Wave realized that there was something terribly wrong here. What could it be? He had to think fast because he didn't have much time left before he would go crashing into the beach. That was it! There was almost no more time left. He saw the waves ahead of him tumble into the sand and get eaten up by the land. Big waves were crashing and disappearing almost instantly. The land had an insatiable appetite. No matter how many waves poured into it, the beach ate them all. His time was fast coming to an end. He wanted to turn back. Little waves, all that was left of the those that had preceded him, came drifting back trying to warn him. "Go back. Go back," they gurgled weakly, their former power spent and gone.

It was too late. The wind, the moon, the waves pushing him from behind made his end inevitable. So this is where it all was leading. For a brief moment he wished that the ocean would have stretched endlessly so that he could go on and on experiencing things forever. He wanted to plead with the sun, but it had gone down; with the moon, but it was too far away; with the people, but they were too excited to listen. There was nothing he could do. He let himself go crashing into the shore amid the excited squeals of the sinking world around him.

"Good-bye, world," Wave cried as he sank into the sand.

"What do you mean good-bye?" the ocean said. "You are not gone. You've just come back to me where you belong."

"But where am I? I can't see me any more."

"You're all one with me again," the ocean replied.

"But, there were so many more things I wanted to see and do."

"You didn't miss a thing," the ocean reassured him. "Let me explain. When you returned to me, you brought with you the memory of all your experiences. When all the other waves sink back into me, they bring with them all their memories. Then, we share all the experiences and memories together. Their experiences become yours and your experiences become theirs. We all become one. Look deep within and you will see now like you never did before."

Wave looked inside and saw giant icebergs floating by. He had never encountered them before while he moved along the surface. But it was happening to him now below the surface even though there were no icebergs to be seen. "This is strange," Wave thought. He looked deeper still and a whole new world opened up before him, filled with whaling ships and schooners, tropical islands and frozen fjords, thatched roof villages and concrete cities. And because all the waves of all times were merged into one, Wave also saw huge lumbering dinosaurs and flying ptero-dactyls. Wave saw everything and felt everything from the very first drop of water that began the ocean until that moment.

Wave finally relaxed and settled comfortably deep within the ocean.

"Oh! One more thing," he suddenly remembered.

"What now?" the ocean asked.

"What about all the things that are yet to happen? Will I miss them?"

"You won't miss a thing," the ocean sighed. "When they happen to me, they will be happening to you."

"Wow!"

It was the first thing and the last thing Wave said.

Moral: We are waves in the ocean of God.

Mysticism, like God, has no religion or denomination.

THE ANT AND THE GRAIN OF SAND

Somewhere along a vast and endless beach, a tiny ant tripped over an even tinier grain of sand and moved it, just barely, from here to there. Did the movement profoundly affect the order of the beach? Did it alter the course of the ocean? Did it impede the rotation of the planet or the direction of the solar system? Did the movement of that tiny grain of sand on that beach impact on the stars or impair the balance of the universe? No. Stars did not fall because of it. Planets did not collide on account of it. The symphony of the universe continued on in spite of it. The cosmos took no account of it.

But God did. For God was in the ant and in the tinier grain of sand.

THE LITTLE BIRD
WHO CRIED

*W*hen Little Bird woke up, the sun was shining brilliantly, fluffy white clouds drifted lazily in the warm summer breeze, and the sweet smells of earth perfumed the orchard where he nested. It was a glorious morning.

He started his day performing his usual morning chores of preening himself and then straightening out his nest before flying off to the bird bath where he bathed daily. The journey took him past a cherry orchard where the trees were heavy laden with delicious fat red cherries and berry bushes filled with succulent wild berries. Next, he flew over a babbling brook whose crystal waters sparkled like diamonds in the sunlight. This was followed by a pass over a field of grain undulating like a giant golden sea. Finally, he swooped down over an array of wild flowers more colorful than a fireworks display, eventually landing ever so gently on the rim of a bright, white marble bird bath.

Unfortunately, when he went to jump into its refreshing waters, he was surprised to discover that there was nothing in it. It was empty and dry. The warm wind and hot sun had taken away all the water, even to the very last drop.

Little Bird didn't know what to make of this strange phenomenon. Nothing like this had ever happened before. There had always been water in the bath. And, it was always clean, cool, and refreshing. Now, there was nothing. Absolutely nothing. Not even dampness on the bottom of the bowl.

He jumped in and squatted down just as he always did, perhaps hoping that the mere repetition of the ritual would somehow miraculously cause the bird bath to fill up with water once again. But, nothing happened.

What would he do now that his daily routine had been thwarted? What could he do? He decided to pretend that there still was water in the bowl so that he could take a bath and get on with his day. He ruffled his feathers, stretched, and shook himself the way he always did. But, he felt no coolness on his body, no relief from the hot sun. It didn't work. Nothing but water would do the trick and he knew it. So, right there, in the middle of the white marble bird bath baking in the sunlight, Little Bird began to cry.

He cried for quite a while before an owl seeing his plight flew down and perched herself on the rim of the bowl.

"Why are you crying?" she asked.

"Because there is no water in the bath," he answered annoyed at her intrusion into his grief. "As you can plainly see."

"I see more than with just my eyes," she replied, not unaware of how the other birds joked about her big eyes.

"What is that supposed to mean?" Little Bird asked impatiently. Having failed to find any solution to his dilemma other than pretending it didn't exist, he preferred to simply wallow in his grief. The owl's interruption was an annoying distraction.

She gave Little Bird a moment to think, but it did no good. When he continued to cry, she asked, "Do you know why there is no water in your bath?"

"I haven't a clue," he replied. "Every day I fly here and every day there's water in the basin and I bathe."

"Then, what do you do?"

"Then I fly off for something to eat."

"Tell me what is it you eat?"

Little Bird became even more impatient with all this questioning. Surely, the owl knew what he ate. The same thing she did, of course.

"I eat cherries and berries from the trees and bushes. And I eat grain from the fields."

"Then what?"

More questions, Little Bird thought. What is all this leading to? How will this fill my bath with water?

"Then, I go to the brook for a drink!" Little Bird's manner was making it abundantly clear that he was in no mood to answer any more foolish questions. The owl was wise enough to see this.

"Let me tell you, my little friend, where the water went. The sun and the wind have taken it away."

"Well, they can just bring it back!" he said imperiously.

"Well, as a matter of fact," she replied mimicking him, "they did."

"What's that supposed to mean? There's no water here." Now, it was his turn to ask questions.

"The sun picked it up," the owl explained, "and the wind carried it away from here." She paused for a moment to let that sink in and then continued. "But, they always give it back. It's just that they put it back some place else."

"Well, they can just put it right back here where they got it!" Little Bird cried. He knew exactly what he wanted and there was no getting away from it. The sooner the owl, the sun, and the wind learned it—or the whole world for that matter—the better.

"They can't," she said.

"Why not?" he asked impatiently.

"Because the moment the sun picks it up the wind moves off with it. It's the nature of things. The sun can't help taking it any more than the wind can help moving it."

"And I can't help crying about it," Little Bird sobbed, dropping big tears into the bird bath. "Tell them to give it back to me."

"They have," the owl continued.

"Nonsense. As you can plainly see there is no water in my bath."

"Not in the bath." She replied turning her eyes toward the fields, "but in the berries you eat and the brook where you drink."

"I don't care about those right now. I care only about my bath. What good are they to me if I can't get to them unless I take my bath first? First I bathe and then I eat." To Little Bird this supposedly made sense. But not to the owl. There was nothing more she could say. So she left.

Little Bird cried himself out of tears and eventually returned home to his nest. He didn't stop to eat at the cherry grove or pick grain from the field or drink from the babbling brook, so great was his grief.

The owl on the other hand went off and gathered enough food to fill twelve baskets. When she finished, she flew to the bird bath and cooled herself off bathing in Little Bird's tears.

THE ELUSIVE BUTTERFLY

I was walking along a country road on a brilliant sunlit afternoon lost in wonder over the beauty of the cloud-dappled sky, the flower-drenched meadow, the delightful antics of playful birds, and the sweet smell of summer in the warm breeze. Then, coming like a jewel to complete the crown was the most remarkable butterfly I had ever seen. It was like none other I, or for that matter, the world, had ever seen before. If the act of love between the sun and the earth is the rainbow, then this butterfly was the living incarnation of that love, for its wings were as if cut out of the rainbow itself and bright as the sun. Were I to look upon the rainbow at that moment, I would surely see the gap where this part of it had broken free and settled tentatively on a flower near me.

I approached it agonizingly carefully so as not to frighten off this incredible creature. It was even more remarkable up close where I could see clearly that its wings were so thin and fine that they were almost transparent. I felt that if I were to attempt to reach out and touch them, they would have no more tangibility than the rainbow itself, and my hand would simply pass through them. So I resigned myself to remain fixed where I stood and observe it as best I could without disturbing it.

The next minute or two were as intellectually rewarding as they were soul filling. I scrutinized carefully everything I could about the magnificent butterfly from its size and shape to its color and behavior so that I could investigate the species further at a later time. I felt a slight pang in my heart when the delightful creature eventually flew off on a strong breeze.

To my surprise and dismay, I discovered that there was no such species of butterfly, either listed in any of the known catalogues or recognized by expert entomologists. A summer of extensive research only confirmed my original discovery. Consequently, I determined to capture the butterfly and reveal the treasure to an unsuspecting world. Armed with a net I returned to the scene of the sighting and waited patiently hoping for its return. My efforts were eventually rewarded, and I captured my prize.

After placing it in a specially prepared cage, I photographed it numerous times, but no matter what I did its wings never appeared in any of the instant prints the camera made. Frustrated and exhausted I retired for the night praying for better luck the next day. The next day, however, my quarry was gone. I could discover no possible way in which the butterfly had escaped. Still, it was gone and that was undeniable. I returned to its haunt once again.

With great good fortune I was able to capture the butterfly once more. This time I placed it in a doubly reinforced cage. Since photographing it was impossible, I carefully sketched it down to the minutest detail. This I mailed post haste to a large university for analysis. The following morning I discovered to my astonishment that my prey had somehow escaped again during the night. This defied all rational explanation. The university responded by calling for photographs to verify the find as anyone could make sketches of spurious finds. Either that, they said, or the impaled corpse of the butterfly itself. Nothing else would suffice.

I thought that to kill such an incredible creature would certainly be a crying shame were it not for the promise that once it made its way into the text books, the butterfly would be named after me, its discoverer. Was the life of this beautiful creature worth the price of my gain? In the end, I felt that it would be fair compensation for my loss.

Once again, I found the butterfly in its familiar haunt waiting for me. It offered no resistance to capture as if it now trusted me, which only served to make its impending sacrifice seem all the more pitiable. Yet, for the sake of knowledge and the exaltation of my name, I knew that the price must be paid. I held the creature's delicate wings against a white cardboard backdrop. It was lovely beyond description. All the more was the pity, I thought, that it would have to forfeit its life because of its rare and unique beauty. After one final sympathetic look, I asked the creature for its forgiveness and impaled it with a sharp needle. At that moment it screamed a terrible heart-rending cry. Then, to my utter amazement, in that same instant the magnificent butterfly disappeared.

I awoke to discover that it had all been a dream—a strange and disturbing dream, the kind that leaves you wondering what it could possibly mean. I wondered what the butterfly meant and what price would I be willing to pay for fame or let others pay for my sake.

I would not have to wonder long, for as I walked along the country road, a butterfly with wings like the rainbow flew out of the field and landed on a flower right in front of me.

What is sometimes deemed virtue may just be the absence of temptation.

THE ORCHID

Once upon a time in the garden of life a new flower sprang from the earth—the orchid. It was an incredibly unique and remarkably beautiful flower, only it didn't know this. It was simply being what it was, a magnificent new flower.

Then, one day, along came a forest fairy who was so enchanted and compelled by its beauty that she immediately reached down and touched the flower so that the orchid was suddenly able to look at itself and regard its own beauty.

"Oh!" the flower exclaimed. And, again, "Oh!" as she contemplated her loveliness and radiance. She found everything about herself interesting and appealing, so much so that for the longest time she couldn't take her eyes off herself. Every bit and part of her was truly special, wonderful, and almost infinitely contemplatable. Then, during a momentary lapse of attention, she noticed a rose growing nearby.

"Oh!" she exclaimed as if startled by the discovery that there could be another flower in the garden.

At first she pondered the rose's own unique color and shape, quite different from her own. She found it both interesting and pleasant. But, while the rose was beautiful and appealing, she did not think that it quite measured up to her own very special beauty and finally told her so.

The comment startled the rose who at that moment was busily engaged in contemplating herself. When she looked over and saw the orchid, she too was taken by its outstanding beauty. At first she was speechless. Then, after she got her wits about her, she said, "But, I smell wonderful!"

The orchid was aghast. Alas, she had no smell whatsoever. This upstart flower had something she didn't have. How could this be? She mulled over the disparity for a long time before she finally commented. "But, my petals are long and graceful while yours are rather short and stubby."

Now it was the rose's turn to stew for a while. "But, my color is far more brilliant and attractive than yours," she cried.

Without even a moment's hesitation, the orchid retorted, "In a gaudy sort of way."

Now the rose's color matched her fury. "You are lackluster and mamby-pamby!"

"And you are disagreeable and prickly. It's no wonder you have so many thorns. To match your personality, no doubt."

The two flowers went at it like this all day long. When the forest fairy saw this, she almost regretted giving the flowers the ability to appreciate their own beauty. She thought of taking the gift away, but that would truly have been a shame since they both still gave her so much pleasure that she continued to feel they deserved the same for themselves. But how could she settle this fairly and amicably?

"I know!" she cried. She waved her magic wand over the vast forest and suddenly there sprang up everywhere a profusion of flowers the likes of which the earth had never seen before. There were pansies, tulips, carnations, daffodils, violets, honeysuckle, chrysanthemums, hydrangeas, and on and on in a near infinite variety of sizes, shapes, colors, and aromas.

"An infinite variety shall make their debate meaningless," the forest fairy smiled at her solution.

"We shall see," said the orchid.

"So we shall," said the rose.

"Yes, we shall," said History.

Moral: This is the story of the birth of the Ego.

FLIGHT OF THE EAGLE

*W*hen baby eagle was born in his mountain aerie, the infinite sky stretched above him, and the vast earth lay as a carpet beneath his feet. His mother told him that he was born midway between heaven and earth and that one day he would have to choose which way he wanted to go. Of course, she knew that he was far too young to understand what she said, but it was necessary for her to plant that particular seed of wisdom at the very beginning of his life, just as it had been done for her and generations of eagles before her.

Custom held that she must give her newborn a name, otherwise she would have no way of calling out to him amid all the other eaglets being born at the time. Her own name was Dawn since she entered life at the very moment of the sun's rising. What name did the heavens have in store for this newborn son of hers? She scanned the heavens and the earth for a sign. Dark clouds were gathering quickly overhead. And, as so often happens at mountain heights, almost without warning lightning flashed, thunder bellowed, and a violent wind whipped through the trees, scattering leaves with a frenzy. "His name shall be Storm," she said.

As quickly as the storm came it passed, and she flew off to find food. Storm watched his mother take off in flight and was anxious to follow her. Besides, the nest was a cold and lonely place without her, so he waddled his way to the edge of the nest. However, he did not have the strength as yet to make it over the top, so he cuddled up and waited.

His first few days were idyllic—eating to his heart's content and basking in the warmth of his mother's wings. Dawn regaled him with fanciful tales of her adventures all of which served to fan the flames of his own desire to set out on his own quests. But she continually warned him that he was not yet ready for it.

One day while she was off hunting, Storm climbed to the top of the nest. Life and adventure were beckoning, and he could wait no longer. Flapping his still immature wings and testing his bravado were dangerous at that height because a sudden gust of wind pushed him over the edge and sent him falling helplessly toward earth.

"Dawn!" "Dawn!" he cried, flapping his wings in a futile attempt to fly. But she was nowhere to be seen. Storm discovered the meaning of terror. His heart beat rapidly, his tiny wings beat furiously, and instinctively he knew that all this spelled catastrophe.

He crashed to the earth with a thud. Pain encompassed his young body like a shroud. He drew in his tiny legs and wings as if to consolidate what little strength he had left. He opened his mouth to call out to his mother, but no matter how hard he tried, he could make no sound at all. He closed his eyes in death.

"Storm!" "Storm!" his mother called shrilly as she flew in circles over the nest. "Storm!" "Storm!" She correctly assumed that he had disregarded her warnings and left the nest prematurely. When she heard no response she presumed that he was dead. Still, she circled over and over again repeatedly calling his name.

Storm lay on a ledge far below the nest. His mother's call had penetrated his numbness and brought him back to consciousness, but he had no strength to call back to her. The ledge had stopped his fall and saved his life, at least what little was left of it. But the sun was setting and it would soon be cold. If his mother didn't find him, he would never survive the night.

Then, from out of nowhere she swooped down onto the ledge where he lay. Her intuition and her eagle eye led her faultlessly to her injured son. He was too happy and too much in pain even to acknowledge her arrival. She nested herself alongside him and cradled him beneath her wings.

Storm was still hurting the next morning, but with his mother beside him he was no longer afraid. At least not until she urged him to move to the edge of the ledge.

"We must return to our nest," she said calmly trying to minimize his already mounting fear.

"Why?" Storm asked. "Why can't we just stay here and make this our home?"

"It is not safe here," she replied.

"Why not?" This made no sense at all. Here or there— what difference did it make? Besides, Storm could not imagine how he would get back to their nest way up above the ledge.

His mother certainly knew that he couldn't fly. That's what got him into trouble in the first place.

"The wind," she said. "One strong gust and it will bounce off against the back of the ledge and blow us all off. We must go back home where it is safe."

"How?"

Storm knew that his mother must realize that he couldn't fly. As a matter of fact, he was quite sure that he didn't ever want to fly. He would just remain in the nest for the rest of his life and let his mother take care of him. But how was he going to get back there?

"You must jump off the ledge," she said.

"You must be joking," Storm shot back. "Listen, I no sooner came into this world than I suffered a great fall. There's no way I want to do that again."

"There's no other way," Dawn said.

"What's to keep me from falling again?"

"Me. I will bear you up on my wings. But, I can't do that unless you get off this ledge.

"I'm afraid," Storm whined.

"Trust me."

Still in pain, Storm inched his way to the edge. Dawn flew overhead beating her wings. Whether it was her flapping that created the wind which forced him over the edge or his own courage that pushed him over the brink, it's impossible to say. In either event, Storm found himself once again in the midst of a disastrous fall.

Dawn swooped under him and caught him on her back. He clutched to it with all the strength he had left and let himself be carried safely home.

Even as he grew, Storm bore the inner scar of his terrible ordeal and secretly resolved to do everything in his power to make sure that he would never again be in danger of a fatal fall. This he did by refusing to venture forth from the nest without the assurance of his mother's presence. Even with her there, he would no sooner drop out of the nest when he would start calling frantically for her help. She patiently indulged him because she realized that he was still suffering from the effects of his fall. But the day would come when he would have to be on his own.

Storm knew from what his mother was teaching him that she would not always be there to protect him. He dreaded the possibility and sought to find some other way to protect himself. The solution came one day when he saw some visitors to the wildlife refuge do a remarkable thing. They tied long cords to their feet and recklessly jumped off a high bridge. The sight so reminded Storm of his own terrifying fall that he was about to cover his eyes when to his amazement he saw that their fall was stopped just short of a catastrophe because they were tethered to the bridge. Not only were they unhurt, but they were daring or foolish enough to go up and do it again and again.

"That's what I must do to make sure that I will not fall and be hurt," Storm said. So over the next several days he carefully gathered vines that grew near his nest and wove them together into a cord. This he fastened to one foot and made his way to the brink. One final test to make sure it would hold and he leaped off into space. His wings were now strong and the wind was gentle and sure so he was borne aloft. It was wonderful. He was flying at last.

He flew in circles over and over again as far as the cord would allow, all the while shrieking happily. When he grew tired of his first day's flight he returned to the nest and wallowed in his accomplishment. The moment his mother returned, he told her animatedly of his adventure, but carefully avoided all mention of the tethering rope.

"Finally!" she exclaimed. "I was beginning to wonder if it would ever come."

The next morning when Storm awoke, Dawn was already gone. He never saw her again. He waited and waited for her to return with food, but when she didn't, hunger drove him from the nest in search of his own. The tethering rope, however, would only let him go so far. But it was enough for now. He would make it longer after he satisfied his appetite.

As the days gathered into weeks, Storm worked on his tethering rope, making it longer and longer. While it allowed him greater movement, it also caused him no small amount of distress as it constantly got tangled up in trees and bushes. Thereafter, his life began to take on a certain rhythm—he would eat his catch of the day and then patiently repair the rope.

Even when Storm was a mature eagle, he never considered flight without the security of his lifeline. Whenever he took it off to repair it, he felt almost naked. It made no difference that other birds hooted at him or called to him to fly off with them. He would go only so far as the tether would allow and no more.

"Let them go where they want," he said. "I go far enough for me." The truth was that he could go only as far as the length of the rope, which was the distance from his nest high up the cliff to just short of the earth far below. In that way, should he ever fall, he would never strike the ground and be killed. It was the price he had to pay, but his life was worth it.

Then, one evening a strange thing happened to Storm. As customary, he preened himself after a long day's work and settled himself down for a long night's rest. Something strange and unaccountable was stirring deep within him. He had been feeling it all day long, but he could make no sense of it. Now, as he readied himself for sleep, the strange sensation was beginning to overwhelm him.

He felt irresistibly compelled to stand up. What was happening? He looked down at the earth far below him, fading in the sunset. A shiver ran up his back. He checked to make sure that his cord was securely fastened to his foot. It was. He looked around his nest wondering if there were some sort of danger lurking there, but there wasn't. What could it be?

When he lifted his head a bit higher he saw the setting sun off in the horizon. It was sinking slowly but surely toward the earth. Then it struck him. In all his evenings he had always been so preoccupied with taking care of his needs before going to sleep that he never bothered to take any real notice of the setting sun. Why he did today was a mystery. But, notice he did, as if for the very first time. He not only noticed the sun—he stared at it with an intensity he had never experienced before. He was overwhelmed by it. His heart stirred in a way it hadn't since his near-fatal fall. There was passion and fire in his look. There was feeling and emotion almost beyond description. There was spellbinding admiration and mesmerizing devotion. Storm was being transfigured by love. He had fallen instantly and irretrievably in love with the sun. It was something he had never experienced before. It transcended everything he had ever known. For the first time in his life he was touched by something that took him beyond even himself.

Yet, while in the throes of ecstasy, there was at the same moment overwhelming dread. With love came the terror of loss. He had discovered his love for the sun, but the sun was about to crash into the earth and die—die in the same way that he almost did. Storm had done what it took to take care of himself. Now he must do whatever it took to save the sun.

There was precious little time left. He had to move quickly. He catapulted himself out of the nest and flew with every ounce of his strength straight toward the sun. If he flew hard enough and fast enough he would make it in time. Then, suddenly, he was stopped abruptly and violently in his flight. He had come to the end of his tether. He flapped his wings frantically but could go no further. The sun was sinking faster. He must act now or it would be the end of everything.

Whether it was Storm's love for the sun or the fear of his own loss that drove him, we shall never know because at that moment he bit through the cord that kept him tethered to the earth and flew off into the sunset. He has not been seen or heard from since.

* * *

It is said by folklorists that Storm reached the sun just in the nick of time. He tied a cord around it, which he secured to his foot, and to this day he keeps it safe from falling and crashing into the earth.

Moral: Ego is the cord we fashion that keeps us earthbound. We must sever ourselves from it if we wish to fly to the sun.

THE MOUNTAIN

A boy stood before the highest, most imposing mountain he had ever seen.

"What are you here for?" he asked.

"What do you say?" the mountain replied.

"To play on," he answered, scrambling up its slopes and sliding down again.

* * *

As a young man he asked the mountain, "What are you here for?"

"What do you say?" the mountain replied.

"To challenge," he shouted and then took on some of its lesser-imposing peaks.

* * *

As a man he asked the mountain, "What are you here for?"

"What do you say?" the mountain replied.

"To conquer!" he cried with a mighty resolve and began his assault on the highest peak. Three times he tried, and three times he was beaten down. On the fourth attempt he made it to the top.

* * *

As an old man, he sat at the foot of the mountain.

"What am I here for?" the mountain asked.

The old man contemplated a long time before answering. "Certainly not as a monument to man's ego. Climbing over anything can never make a small man big no matter how many mountains he conquers.

"Then, what am I here for?" the mountain repeated.

The old man looked at its snow-capped peaks crowned with a halo of clouds and its emerald green mantle with flower-decked train. He listened to its cavernous roar with every thunder clap and its idle chatter in every babbling brook. He reflected on how it gave shelter to the forest creatures—the deer, the bear, the rabbit, and even the lowly field mouse; how it offered nurture to the birds of the air and the fish in its lakes; and how it gave to man every manner of consolation from livelihood to contemplation.

"What am I here for?" the mountain asked again.

The old man said not a word. Instead, he rose and took off his shoes.

"Now you know," the mountain said.

Moral: Mountains are for majesty.

THE BOY AND THE ELEPHANT

A boy wanted to get an elephant to move from one side of a field to the other. The elephant, however, was content to remain where it was, grazing at its leisure. He pondered the dilemma for a while before he thought of a plan. He gave the elephant a banana to eat which the great beast liked and quickly devoured. He then took another banana and threw it a stone's throw across the field. The elephant slowly and ponderously lumbered over to it and ate it. He threw another banana and another until the elephant crossed the field.

Moral: You can move anything if you find the right bait. The trick is never to throw it out of sight.

THE FLOWER

*O*ne day while walking through a field a man chanced upon a flower, the first flower he had ever set eyes upon in his entire life. He immediately broke forth into song.

> Oh, thou beauteous star
> fallen gift from afar
> diamond bright

> dispelling night
> oracle sweet
> with fragranced meat
> for thee no mere mortal nod
> for thou art truly, living god.

He could not resist its allure, its captivating presence, its unshakable grasp upon his heart. He plucked the flower and lovingly carried it home with him.

Charmed by its beauty and captivated by its sweet fragrance, he determined to know all that there was to know about this remarkable treasure. Where did it come from? How did it come by such great beauty? What was the source of its spell-binding fragrance? It was love that urged him on and an insatiable appetite that drove him.

He examined the flower carefully, methodically, and meticulously. He studied books and read journals. He attended workshops, seminars, and institutes. He got a bachelor's degree, then a master's, and finally a doctorate. He became a world-renowned scholar. There was nothing about flowers he did not know, lecture on, or write about. When it came to flowers, he had no equal on earth.

Yet, in spite of all this, he was sad and unsatisfied. What more could he do than he had already done? What more could he possibly learn when he felt certain that he knew all that there was to know? What was missing? What was wrong?

He carried his concern to a field laden with flowers that he himself had planted. Standing in their midst as the sun sank slowly in the horizon, he saw the evening star rise for the very first time in his life. It was brilliant and beautiful and captivating. He stared in rapt wonder. A song broke forth from his mouth.

Then, the revelation came to him. He had lost the poetry of flowers. The song was gone.

The man sat in that field all night long staring at the stars. When the dawn came, he resolved that he would never, ever become an astronomer.

Moral: Explanations are never enough for the soul.

God is to be found more in the common touch than in the pursuit and acquisition of knowledge, for whatever separates you from your fellow man distances you from God.

THE FROG KISSER

Once upon a time there was a very special teacher who loved all her pupils and whose pupils all loved her in return. Now that doesn't mean that she wasn't ever strict or demanding when the situation called for it, because she was. But the children all knew that deep down she really and truly cared for them. There was nothing she wouldn't do to help them learn and grow.

One summer evening, one of her young pupils, after finishing his chores, noticed her strolling leisurely along the path that circled the village pond. Curious like all young boys, he decided to follow her, but carefully so as not to be seen. When she sat down on a bench near the water, he hid in nearby bushes. He almost laughed out loud when a big bull frog jumped out of the pond and landed directly in front of her. He expected the teacher to scream and run away the way the girls in his class would, but instead she just sat there calmly and watched it. After a while it seemed to him like she was actually talking to it. Imagine talking to a frog.

It never occurred to him that he talked to his dog and cat and even his pet turtle. Well, if he had thought of it, he would have said that they were his pets and not some big, ugly, bull frog from a pond. He would have thought it if he had a minute more. But, just then, the teacher did a startling thing. She got up from the bench, picked up the frog, and kissed it.

Before he could scream out and warn her that she'll get warts, an amazing thing happened. The frog changed into a handsome young prince. He couldn't believe his eyes. He rubbed them and rubbed them just to make sure of what he was seeing. It was a prince all right. The young man then bowed deeply before the teacher, kissed her on both cheeks, and walked away bidding her farewell.

By the time the boy came to his senses, the teacher was gone and the sun had set. He wanted to hurry off and tell someone about what happened, but who would believe it? People would say he was only making things up the way that boys often do. After a while he wasn't sure himself about what he had seen, so he decided to follow her again.

It wasn't until a couple of weeks later that the teacher returned to the pond. Once again she sat on the bench and waited. Sure enough another bull frog leapt from the water and hopped over to her. Once again she spoke kindly to it for a while. Then, like before, she reached down, picked it up, and kissed it. Suddenly, a beautiful princess stood before her. The princess curtsied politely, kissed the teacher on both cheeks, and left. The poor boy was caught between utter amazement and an overwhelming desire to see if he could do the same thing. As soon as the teacher left, he sat on the bench and waited. Before long a frog jumped out of the water and approached him. Summoning up all his courage, he snatched it up and kissed it.

"Ribbit," the frog said.

He immediately dropped the fog and wiped the taste of it from his lips. "I'm going to get warts," he cried.

When he saw the next day that he didn't get warts, he decided to try again. This time he wanted to make sure he did everything exactly the same way as his teacher did. He came to the pond at sunset. Waited for a frog. Talked to it for a while, even though he felt stupid doing it. Then, he kissed it.

"Ribbit," the frog said again.

"I'm going to get warts, for sure this time," he cried.

When he didn't, he tried it a few more times, but to no avail. So, he decided to follow his teacher one last time. That evening as the sun was setting and she sat on the familiar bench near the pond, he watched as she once again kissed a frog and it turned into a beautiful princess.

After the princess left, he burst out of the bushes and confronted the teacher. When he told her how he had tried and tried kissing he didn't know how many frogs and nothing happened, she could only laugh politely.

"Better be careful," she teased. "You might get warts."

However, when she saw how truly frustrated the poor boy was, she had to relieve his misery so she explained. "You saw me kiss a frog and watched it turn into a princess and you wanted to do the same thing. I suppose you think it's a trick or magic. It is not a trick, my boy. Nor is it magic. What you must learn is that you can't kiss a frog to get a princess or you'll just get a frog. When you kiss a frog just because it is a frog, then you will get a princess. Or a prince. It doesn't really matter."

"That's amazing," the boy replied. "How did you discover that?"

"It was easy," she laughed. "I was once a frog."

Moral: When you love something for what it is and not for what you want it to be, you will both be rewarded.

Love a frog just because it is a frog and you both benefit. Love a frog because you expect a prince and you'll get warts.

———————

THE KISS

I saw a mother kiss her infant child and thought to myself—no one ever kisses me.

I saw two lovers kissing beneath a tree and cried to myself—no one ever kisses me.

I saw friends part with a kiss and grieved not for them but for me—because no one ever kisses me.

I saw a traveler extend a kiss and I died a little more. No one ever kisses me, I mourned.

But then, the traveler did a curious thing. After the first kiss, she kissed again and said, "This one's from your uncle."

Could someone send a kiss? Somewhere an uncle did, and I thought to myself, What is a kiss?

What is a kiss if not the breath of life given from one to another? All of me wishes to give life to all of you. All of you wishes to give life to all of me. We pass it from lips to lips, mouth to mouth. It is a sharing in the essential kiss, the fundamental kiss from which all others derive their power and meaning. "Let there be life!"

A kiss is simply an outward sign meant to convey someone's inner desire to give life. Therefore, kisses have to go beyond mouth to mouth and lips to lips. Whatever conveys the message of life is a kiss. A hug, a handshake, and even a wave are all kisses. A greeting card, a gift, and a smile are kisses.

When that traveler conveyed a kiss, she carried the wish of life from a loving person to a loved one. I pondered these things as I walked along.

Suddenly, a bird's sweet song drew my attention and at once I felt kissed. Nearby, a wild tiger lily waved at me and again I felt kissed. Now, there were kisses everywhere. The evergreen sent its fresh scent, the bee hummed a tune, and the wind ran its fingers through my hair, and I was covered with kisses. At last I have come to know that the kisses never stop coming. They are infinite.

They are infinite because there are infinite messengers. Like that traveler. Sent from the Ultimate Lover.

Never again dare I say, "No one ever kisses me."

THE LAWN AND THE BOULDER

*H*aving moved to an arid rural area, a woman and her husband decided to enhance their property by growing a luxurious green lawn. It was long and painstaking work, but they finally achieved their goal. The meticulously manicured grass lay like a rich carpet around the house. In the midst of the desert, it was a marvel to behold and the pride of the community.

Then one morning a huge boulder broke loose from its mountain perch and rolled down, landing in the very middle of the new lawn. It was big, ungainly, and awful to look at, and the couple wanted to have it removed but were told that the project was too unwieldy and costly to be worthwhile. They could only mourn their unhappy fate.

The children however found it to be a delight. It was a mountain for playing King of the Mountain, a fort to be defended against all comers, a hide-out, a slide, a leaning post, a basking place, and a space ship from a distant planet. Since they couldn't remove it, the couple decided to decorate around it. They made it the center piece of a rock garden and planted all manner of local shrubs and wild flowers around it.

In the end it turned out to be just as good as the marvelous green lawn. Some said even better.

Moral: An open heart and mind can reshape any tragedy.

I AM A MEAL

I am a meal. Sometimes I am just the first course, the antipasto before the main plate. A light and airy snack, satisfying but not too filling. Enough to whet the appetite yet leave the promise of more to come.

Sometimes I am a part of the main course. At times I am the meat—rich, nourishing, and life giving. I am grateful that the game gave its life for me so that I might give my life to others. At other times I am the potatoes—the vegetables that round out our additional needs and desires. They are what add dimension and color to the plate and to life. And at times I am just plain bread. Not exciting but necessary, wholesome and filling.

Then, there are times when I am dessert. Sweet and fluffy, satisfying and delicious. Never enough by itself. Yet an occasional, necessary embellishment to the ordinary.

I am a meal, a part of life's banquet. And to those who come to my table I must needs tell you that I am almost never a full meal, at least not all the time. But, with my sincerest blessings I invite you to take what I have to offer—and bon appetit!

Good people are like good soups, stews, and spaghetti sauce. They're a wonderful blend that gets even better with age.

THE CROOKED RIVER

*I*n ancient Asia Minor a young student asked his teacher, "Why must I wait before I can fulfill the passionate dreams that burn within me?"

The old man nodded knowingly, for he had heard the familiar question many times over the years. It was the age-old question of youth, but this time it stirred him to his soul for he knew that it would be the last time he would have to answer it. So he led the boy up a high mountain where the view of the land they lived in was as wide and clear as it was breathtaking.

"Tell me what you see, boy," he said, his arm sweeping across the horizon.

"I see a great land nestled beneath these mountains extending to the sea," the boy answered.

"Look again," the old man sighed, "and tell me more."

The youth turned toward the vista again. "I see a blue ocean and a green valley with a crooked river running through it."

"Now, keep your eyes fixed on what you see, neither turning nor blinking until all that you are looking at has burned its impression upon your mind."

The boy did as he was instructed until he could close his eyes and see the panorama as if they were still open. "It is done, master," he said, and the two moved on.

The old man led the youth to where the crooked river began. "Tell me what you see," he said.

"I see waters coming together into a stream," he replied.

"Look again and tell me more."

The boy scanned quickly once again and answered, "Just so."

"Now, we wait," the old man sighed as he eased himself on a rock. The boy sat on the grass at his feet staring distractedly. They sat there for a long time before the old man spoke again.

"Tell me what you see."

"I see tall trees full of leaves. I see bushes and grass and a bright clear stream."

"Look again and tell me more." Impatient to move on, the boy looked closer and harder. "I see clouds floating across the sky. I see birds nesting in the trees. I see a rabbit hiding in the grass." But, seeing no change in his mentor's demeanor, he quickly added, "And bright colorful flowers."

The old man merely nodded and sat there quietly. When he asked his question a third time, the boy answered curtly, "Just so."

Still they waited until the boy asked his mentor, "Master, tell me what you see."

"I see the wind and crickets and a home-cooked meal."

"Sir, how can you see the wind?"

"Look around you with all your senses," he replied. "See more than just what your eyes light upon. Look beyond the apparent. See with not just the body but also the mind."

Again the boy looked around. This time he said, "I see the wind with my skin. I see the crickets with my ears. I see the meal with my nose. And I see the beginning of a river with my mind."

The old man rose and moved on. The boy also saw happiness within his spirit.

When they came to a waterfall they stopped.

"Tell me what you see."

The boy looked closely. "I see water cascading down the mountain with great power."

"Good," the old man replied. "You are learning. You see more than just water falling. Now, tell me where does this power come from?"

"From the stream itself," he answered quickly.

"Then why did you say it has power now and not before?"

The boy thought for a moment. He was learning to see with his mind. "The drop in the earth gave the water its power."

"You have spoken well. Now see more and tell me whence came this water."

The boy answered, "From the rain and melting snow."

"So you see its power comes not just from itself but elsewhere—the earth and the sky."

"It is just so, master," the youth replied pleased at how quickly he was learning.

"Look again now and continue to see more."

The young man looked above and below the waterfall. "I see a rapidly flowing stream surrounded by shrubs, flowers, and moss above the falls and a blue-green lake below in the midst of an abundance of trees."

"Is anything growing where the water is falling?"

"No, master."

"Why is this so when there is so much water to be had?"

"Because it passes much too quickly."

"Now look with your mind at what you have seen."

After a brief pause the youth replied, "What passes quickly leaves little evidence of itself behind." He was pleased with his answer.

"And what of power?"

He pondered a bit longer before answering. "The power of things," he said thoughtfully, "comes not from the thing alone but also from above and around." He was beginning to get the idea. He looked up and down again and saw more. "Above the falls where the stream passes quickly, it has time to give only a little nurture to the land adjacent to it. So there are just shrubs and moss to benefit from it. Below the falls there is a great pool. While there seems to be little power left here, it has actually spread its strength throughout the surrounding countryside. Hence, the tall trees and the thick woods."

"Good." The old man smiled for the first time. "Tell me more."

"Men do not have power from themselves alone. It also comes from above and around them. When their strength seems to be at its greatest and moving forcefully, it does little good for what is around them. When it is settled and peaceful, it nurtures and sustains life far and wide."

"Very good," the teacher replied and moved on.

The river resumed its course at the far side of the lake and wound a slow, tortuous path through the valley. The old man moved as slowly and deliberately as the sluggish waters and just as quietly. Here there was no deafening roar of cascading waters, no splashing and churning clamor of rapids beating their way over rocks and around bends, no babbling brooks urging it onward. There was no sound from the river and no comment or observation from the mentor. Slowly and aimlessly the three of them continued onward.

At long last the youth spoke. "Master, where are we going?"

"To Ephesus," he replied.

"But the city is not that far to the west," the boy protested. "Why are we following this river?"

"Because like us it, too, is going there."

"But its path is painfully slow and aggravatingly crooked. Why don't we just go directly there instead?" he pleaded impatiently.

"Because there is still much to learn this way." The old man found a fallen tree trunk and sat upon it like a bishop on his throne. "Tell me what you have seen."

The boy thought for a while before answering. "I have seen a brook rush into a stream and the stream into a river. I have seen the river fall into a lake and the lake send it on its way again. I have seen moss grow where trees cannot and the earth fruitless where the waters rushed past."

"And of our wandering, tell me, why does the river twist and turn when it too wishes to go directly to the sea like us?"

The boy closed his eyes and reflected on their journey. "At every twist the earth put an obstacle in its path so the river had to change its course if it wished to move on."

"Was this good or bad?" the teacher asked.

"Bad," the boy quickly replied.

"How so?"

"Because it thwarted the river's goal."

"But what of the earth's goal?"

"How so?" the boy asked.

"When the river made its way around an obstacle what did you see?"

Once again he closed his eyes and reflected. "Wherever the river ran, there were fields and farms rich with produce. There were trees and groves and vines ripe for harvest. Where the river ran, there was life. Where it didn't, there wasn't."

"So tell me what you have learned."

"From the river and the earth I have learned that there are other purposes than just one's own. I see that what appears to be an obstacle may also be an opportunity. Each obstacle in the river's path led it to bring life to a land which otherwise might have been arid and lifeless."

"So the obstacles are not so bad, after all."

The boy pondered these things as they resumed their journey. At last, they arrived at the great city of Ephesus. The old man brought the boy to where the river ran into the sea.

"Tell me what you see."

The boy looked back to the mountains and closed his eyes. Once again he saw the sight of what the old mentor had asked him to burn into his memory at the beginning of their journey. But, now he saw more. Much more than before. More than just with his eyes.

"I see that life does not rush quickly to its goal as I once wanted it to."

"Tell me more."

The boy faced the sea where the sun was setting. "I see that more is accomplished in leisure than in haste. I see that in the end all rivers make their way to the sea."

"Tell me about the river."

In his mind the boy saw the river twisting and turning its arduous way to the sea. He thought of the countless bends and turns along the way, the many obstacles that caused so many diversions, and the immensely wide area that became fruitful because of all this. "I see that where obstacles abound, there does life even more abound."

"You have learned well from the river," the old man said.

"Good master, tell me. What is the name of the river?"

"It is called the Meander."

And so it has been called to this day.

SACRAMENTS

She stood immobile, spellbound by the wondrous beauty of the magnificent forest that surrounded and embraced her. The distant snow-capped mountains belying their nature were like a fur wrap making her feel warm and comfortable. The lustrous green mantle of trees and shrubs vibrated with richness and life. The spring flowers strewn over the countryside were like gemstones fallen from the arms of some lighthearted wood nymph unconcerned about this petty loss from her bountiful treasure. Birds flew, deer gamboled, rabbits raced, squirrels explored, and bees hummed in this enchanting and mesmerizing symphony of nature.

She experienced the soul-filling richness of it all, and yet it made her strangely sad.

"Will this all pass away?" she asked the wind. If she could, she would remain there forever. This was treasure beyond reckoning, wealth beyond price. To leave such treasure would be inconceivable. To lose such treasure would be unforgivable.

A voice replied. "It can never be lost."

She was startled by the response. Who had heard her heart's soulful quest? She looked and there was no one around. No one except the forest itself.

"Why is that?" she asked. "How can you speak with such certitude?"

"Even if it were all to pass away in the beat of a hummingbird's wing, it would still be here in me," the voice said.

"Who are you," she queried.

"I am at your very feet. At your disposal, so to speak."

She looked down and saw a wonderful mirror lake stretching before her.

"How can you be so certain?" she repeated.

"I will show you," the lake responded. "In the blink of an eye, all that you see around you will be gone. There will be no mountains or trees. There will be no more clouds or flowers or animals. It will all be gone. All you have to do is close your eyes."

She closed her eyes.

"Now, when you open them look down into my face." This, too, she did.

"Tell me what you see."

"I see mountains and hills. I see the clouds and trees and flowers."

"As I said, even if all that surrounds you should pass away, they continue to be in me."

How wonderful, she thought. And how true. "But," she wondered, "if they are no longer there, then you can no longer reflect them."

"Only on the surface," was the lake's strange reply. "Their impression still remains deep within me. Once I have seen the mountain, it remains within me. Once I have seen the sun, the moon, and stars, they remain in me. The deer and the rabbit, the crow and the butterfly, the rain and the rainbow are forever stored in the heart of me. For you to see them in me you must look beyond the surface. You must have deeper sight."

"Your truth is truly wonderful," the woman cried. "However, I fear that it is not enough." She hesitated before speaking again, afraid that the mere mention of her doubt would cause her to lose the treasure she had so recently found. But, unless she owned her doubt, how could she ever lay hold of the treasure? "What will happen when you pass away?"

There was a long silence before the lake spoke again, its voice like the sigh of a summer breeze. "I can never pass away."

The woman waited, not wanting to give offense. She had come this far. Honesty would not let her stay the final query. "What if you were to dry up? What if you were to be drained until there is nothing left. Then what?"

"All of us shall still continue to live, to be."

"How?"

"Have you not been listening? Have I not told you that there is more to me than just the surface of me? All that surrounds me is a part of me. It is in all of me and in every part of me. You see the sky in me and well you should, for it is on the surface of me. But the entire sky is also in my every drop of water. All of it in the tiniest part of me. When the deer comes to drink, I give it the sky. Even if the sky or I should never again be here, we are already in the deer. When the deer gives birth, we are in its young. When the deer grows old and dies we are in the earth. The deer is my sacrament. The earth is my sacrament. When the wind blows over me and claims a part of me, I am in the wind. The wind is my sacrament. The flower that admires itself before me, the fish that swims through me, the spider that races over me, all that find nurture or seek shelter or simply pass me by, all become my sacraments. We can never pass away. We are multiplied a thousand fold. A million fold. We are immortal."

Such an amazing revelation! This knowledge was even more wondrous than the beautiful panorama that stretched before her. She had come to learn that in the beauty of the earth there is inestimable wealth. But in the beauty of truth, there is immortality.

The next step was hers to take. She took it. She stepped up to the lake and gave it her reflection.

––––––––––

Since God is spirit, he is simple and indivisible. This means that God does not come in degrees. Wherever God is, he is present in his fullness. On God's part, it is all or nothing.

THE SHADOW

"*W*hat is it you want from me?" the Great Wizard asked.

"I want to get rid of my shadow."

"Why?"

"Because it is dark, black, and ominous."

"That's because it's your shadow."

"I know that. I still don't like it. I find it depressing and degrading to have something beneath me follow me around wherever I go."

"Have you tried doing anything about it?" he asked indulgently.

"Of course I have. But what can I do? I tried staying out of the light—all light—but if I find the darkness of my shadow depressing, imagine what it was like staying out of the light altogether."

The wizard nodded knowingly but said nothing, as if expecting me to continue. So I did.

"Would you believe I even tried blowing it up, I was so exasperated? Of course, it simply reappeared at the bottom of the hole I made."

This made the wizard laugh. I had to admit that retelling it did make me seem foolish.

"That wasn't all," I continued. "I was determined not to let my shadow get the best of me. After all, I was intelligent, wasn't I?"

It was a rhetorical question but the wizard answered it anyway. "It would seem so," he said. I wasn't sure how he meant that. Nevertheless, I continued.

"I thought I had solved the problem by never looking down. As far as I was concerned, if I didn't see it, it didn't exist."

"Spoken like a true ostrich," he said. But, before I could object, he added, "And then what happened?"

"Well, for one thing, people began avoiding me because they thought I was stuck up. And for another, I couldn't avoid my shadow appearing on walls or trees or anything else that stood up in front of me. It was hopeless,"

"Then why did you come to me?"

"Well, I guess you're my last hope."

"You still want to get rid of your shadow?" he asked almost disbelievingly.

"I do. I don't want there to be any kind of a shadow about me."

The wizard eyed me carefully as if gauging my resolve in this matter. From the desperate look on my face, he must have assessed that I would be willing to do anything. I would.

"There is something, but it is so drastic that I hesitate to mention it."

"Just name it," I said eagerly.

"There is a potion you can take."

"It's guaranteed to make my shadow disappear."

"Yes."

"Then give it to me."

Before the wizard would give me that powerful potion, he explained why it was so drastic a measure.

That was many long years ago. Today, I look back on all of that and laugh. Beneath me my shadow laughs with me. I have learned to live with it, after all. After all, I felt that my life was worth it.

———

The greater the light side of us is, so also must the dark side be, for how can we know the light except for the dark?

HOW THE SUNFLOWER GOT ALL ITS SEEDS

One morning a flower opened her two eyes and discovered the sun. She was dazzled by its beauty and on fire with its radiance. Each day she rejoiced in its brilliance. But each night she wept at her loss.

"I can't take my eyes off of you," she sighed. "And I can't bear the thought of losing you every night."

"The more you love me," the sun whispered soothingly to her, "the more eyes you shall have. The more eyes you have, the more you will have to remember me by at night. Then, every seed you produce will be a memory of me."

So the sunflower grew many eyes and has many seeds.

Moral: Memories are the seeds of love.

SUGAR AND SALT

When sugar is added to food, it draws attention to itself. When salt is added, it brings out the flavor of the food. We are called to be the salt and not the sugar of the earth.

TWO TREES

*T*wo trees grew up together side by side. The one seemed frivolous when it decided to grow as many branches as it possibly could. "I just want to spread out as much and as far as I can. I want to have branches and twigs and leaves everywhere," it said. "What about you?"

The other tree seemed far more serious. "You will spread yourself far too thin," he said. "I will put all my efforts into just one or, at most, two firm and sturdy branches. That's all that's really necessary."

So the two trees grew and did as they had planned, the one with branches spreading everywhere, the other with only two strong offshoots. The winds came and the storms lashed. The frivolous tree lost countless branches, leaves, and twigs. The serious tree stood firm against all the onslaughts.

Then one day there came an ice storm. The weight was too much for the serious tree which lost both its branches and eventually died. While the frivolous tree lost many of its branches, some of them managed to survive and so, too, did the tree.

THE WORD

*T*he master asked his student to tell him the one word that contained all the wisdom of the universe. The student thought deeply. Minutes passed. Then hours. Hours passed into days and weeks and months. At the end of a year the student stood mute before the master.

"You have answered correctly," the master replied.

Moral: Silence is the wisdom of the universe.

———————

When we can't see the truth for the language, we are not open to the truth. Only a true gemologist sees the diamond beneath the carbon. Words are merely the clothes we put on ideas and as happens with all our clothes—fashions change. We must look deeper.

———————

I SAW A HAT

I saw a hat and put it on. I thought it a handsome hat, but it made others laugh, so I took it off.

I saw a wooly coat and put it on. It was big and fuzzy and warm which pleased me. But others disapproved, so I took it off.

I saw a smock and tried it on. It was durable and practical. The others approved, but it didn't fit me, so I took it off.

I saw a pair of shoes. Then another and another and another. They all fit and they all didn't, if you get my drift.

So I decided to wear nothing. Nothing at all.

Now, nobody sees me. No one at all.

Except God and me.

Moral: If clothes do not make the man, does the body?

THE STREET VENDOR

A street vendor wound his way through the city streets, his cart laden with the produce of the season. As he hawked his wares, a slow but steady stream of women and children meandered out of their homes and yards and gathered round his carousel of delights.

"I have potatoes. I have tomatoes. I have onions and peppers," he cried. "There is lettuce round and firm. And green peas soft and tender. I have snow-white cauliflower and deep black eggplants." He sang more than shouted and like a maestro before an orchestra he gestured, pointing here and holding aloft there, while the audience bravoed with their ohhs and ahhs and demanded encores by buying his goods.

In the midst of this commerce, a boy stepped forward and asked him if he had any watermelon. "I have apples and oranges," he answered, "If desserts are your desire."

"I don't want apples or oranges," the boy pouted. "I like watermelon."

"It is not time yet for watermelon, my boy," the vendor said. "When the time comes, be assured that we will both have them."

"But I want it now," the boy cried.

Never one to deny a potential customer, the huckster promised that when he returned the next day the boy would have his watermelon but on the condition that, if he took the trouble to find one, the boy must take the time to eat it.

"No problem," the boy said. "I just love watermelon."

True to his word, the next day the vendor came calling and the people came buying.

"Where's my watermelon?" the boy shouted, not seeing any on his cart.

"I am a man of my word," the vendor said. "And you must be a man of your word."

The boy was flattered that the vendor would refer to him as a man. "Give me the watermelon and I will eat it," he boasted to the crowd of onlookers.

The man took off his cart a green ball no bigger than the size of his fist. "Here's your watermelon," he announced.

"That's no watermelon," the boy protested.

"Oh, but it is," the man replied and the crowd nodded in agreement. "Like you, it is just not full grown yet. You can't rush the melon, and you can't rush the man. Now take and eat," he said holding it out to the boy.

The boy hoped that it would taste like a full grown watermelon but it didn't. It tasted raw and bitter. With every bite he made a sour face to the great amusement of the crowd.

"Learn from the Good Book, my boy," the vendor said. "To everything there is a season. When you are ready and the watermelon is ready, that will be the time for feasting."

Moral: Everything in its time.

THE BAG LADY'S SECRET

*I*t had all become just too much to bear. For the life of her she couldn't say precisely when it all started to turn bad. It was gradual, like some kind of terminal disease that creeps up on you. Even though it gives warning signs of its presence, you ignore them, either because you tell yourself it's nothing but nerves or you're too afraid to find out the truth. Not that it would have made any difference either way. "Damn the torpedoes! Full speed ahead," had become her motto, and nothing could stop her once she got rolling.

Not husband. Not children. And as it turned out, not even career. She had simply become her own person—first, last, and foremost. No barefoot and pregnant housewife for her, even though at one time her only aspiration was to be a loving wife. Not a housewife. She never had any intention or pretensions about marrying a house. No Mammasita for her either. Sitting around all day long watching soaps and gorging herself on candy and pizza as kids climbed all over her was not her idea of motherhood, even though at one time she did picture herself as a happy suburban mother with a station wagon load of beautiful all-American kids. Nor a sweat shop slave satisfied with minimum wage. Nor a career woman controlled by some megalithic organization moving its "executives" around like pawns on a chess board. She had simply become her own woman.

When it started she really couldn't say. Was it because of a book she read, a program she saw on television, a movie, a lecture, or an article in *Woman's Day?* What did it matter now that her life had come apart. This is what it all boiled down to. This is where it all led—to a park bench at Belvista Lookout. There was a joke about it among the locals. They would accent the out in Lookout because it had been used a few times for suicides.

It's all in the way you say it, she thought. Or in the way you live it for that matter. The same thing can mean different things to different people. She saw herself as providing for the kids, but they saw it as neglect and were insistent on getting away for college. There was nothing to make them want to stay at home. She saw herself as business partner as well as spouse. Her husband saw her as competitor and rival. He said he would have preferred infidelity, given the choice. It was probably a cover-up for his own infidelity. Her boss didn't care what she called it. He just fired her.

Which was why she found herself at Belvista Lookout. She wore her depression like a shroud. Not even the beautiful view from the Lookout could raise her fallen spirit. If anything, the contrast only heightened her despondency. If depressed people were supposed to see all this magnificent beauty and take heart in knowing that there is still a beautiful world out there waiting for them, they could also see by contrast how ugly their own world had become. After all, does an ugly woman find hope in knowing that there are beautiful woman around? Is a poor man encouraged by other men striking it rich? What did the Bible say? "It's all a chase after wind."

A fart is more like it. Maybe that's what Ecclesiastes meant but was too dignified to say it. Or uptight. Or hemmed in by rules, expectations, and conventions. Well, she had come to hate them all. They were what got her here. She's wasn't afraid to say it. She stood up and faced it almost defiantly. "Shit!" She yelled it full-throated and wholeheartedly. The magnificent panorama absorbed it without even so much as a ruffled leaf. So much for shit.

"Oh, what's the use," she muttered. "If I'm half the woman I've pretended to be—then just do it." She parodied the local humor. "Look out below. Here I come." How appropriate that her parting shot would be a stab at humor. Life was a joke.

Just as she made her move she saw it. It was lying there at the side of the bench as if it had fallen from someone's pocket. It was a wallet. It looked weather-worn and battered. It was probably abandoned—thrown there by some other hopeless soul as a last testimony of an empty life.

But it wasn't empty. At least not the wallet. Something was sticking out, barely noticeable but noticeable nonetheless. She bent over and picked it up. To all appearances it was a derelict wallet except for one thing. Sticking out of the billfold section was a lottery ticket. Probably dated, she thought. Just my luck.

Surprisingly, it wasn't dated. It was for Saturday's lottery. Twenty-five million dollars. There was a time when she thought that money would solve all her problems. Then she discovered that the more money she made, the bigger her problems got. At some point the problems outran the affluence, and money no longer mattered.

She was about to put the wallet on the bench and resume her course when she was startled by someone shouting, "That's mine!" She turned to see an unkempt and unsightly woman rushing toward her pointing her finger at the wallet.

"That's mine," she repeated in her face.

Marybeth winced. She's lying, no doubt. So, who cares? Why not let her have it?. But, the thought triggered a deep-seated conditioned response, "Says you. Prove it!"

"It's got a lottery ticket in it."

"You could have seen that."

The poor woman looked dumbfounded. She made as if to reply and instead started rummaging through the dirty, old shopping bag she was carrying. Still searching she said, "I'll trade you for it."

"Trade me? Don't make me laugh. What could you possibly have that I would want."

"I know I don't look like much and I don't have much, but I do have something worth trading that lottery ticket for."

This is intriguing, Marybeth thought. Why not indulge her? After all, she didn't have a deadline for committing suicide. How strange. She never thought of it before. Deadline. The line beyond which there was only death. There was a deadline waiting for her. It was the edge of the cliff.

"Are you interested?" The bag lady broke into her thoughts.

"Tell me what you've got."

She pulled out an apple all wrapped in cellophane. Marybeth couldn't help but laugh out loud. "Who are you supposed to be—Apple Annie?"

Suddenly, there was a gleam in the old lady's eye. Or was it the sunlight playing tricks? "My apple is better than any of hers."

"You mean if I eat this one I will fall into a deep sleep until a handsome young prince comes to kiss me?" Her tone was just lighthearted enough not to sound too cynical.

The old lady cast a sly look toward the vista and back at her. "If that's what you want," she answered, "I'm afraid this is not the apple for you."

Marybeth had no intention of ever eating the apple. God only knows where the old lady got it. Besides, the hand that held it out was clothed in a dirty, worn-out glove with all her fingertips protruding. She couldn't imagine taking anything that came from that cruddy bag and dirty hand. It was probably lethal.

As if reading her thoughts, the bag lady said, "Don't worry. It won't kill you."

"I'm not afraid of dying" she shot back and immediately caught the lie. She had read about suicides who were concerned about how they would look when their body was discovered. How strange. Here she is willing to commit suicide and on her way there she's reluctant to eat an unwashed apple. Still, she was not about to share her life or thoughts with this complete stranger. Nervously, she changed the subject.

"This lottery ticket could be very lucky. I could win twenty-five million dollars with it. That apple of yours would have to be something very special to make me want to give up that possibility."

"It's called a Heart of Christ Apple."

"That's blasphemous!" Marybeth shouted with contempt.

"Why? Why is it blasphemous? If the Italians can make a wine called 'Tears of Christ' because it's so good it makes them cry, and the Germans a wine so sweet that they call it 'Blessed Mother's Milk,' why can't we have an apple called 'Heart of Christ'?"

For a bag lady she's pretty knowledgeable, Marybeth thought. "OK. I'll concede the point. But, why Heart of Christ?"

"That's a secret."

"Well, are you going to tell me?" Marybeth smirked, fully expecting to be let in on the big deal.

"If I tell you, then it's not a secret, is it?"

Annoyed and even outraged, Marybeth let her emotions get the best of her. "You expect me to give you a lottery ticket worth twenty-five million dollars for a stupid apple and you won't even tell me why? You're crazy. And if I do, I'm crazy."

"Look at it this way," the bag lady continued. "What are your chances of winning the lottery? Here I'm offering you a very special apple, maybe even a magic apple, in place of a pipe dream. What is it they say, 'One in the hand is worth two in the bush?' Besides, you don't look like the type of person who needs it. Look at me. Why not give me a chance? You may be getting more than you imagine."

Marybeth looked at the bag lady for the first time. She was a pitiful sight. Her face and clothes were dirty beyond description. Almost excessively so. Her hair was disheveled to the point where it would take a rake rather than a comb to straighten it out. Her coat had every appearance of coming from a Goodwill handout—ten years ago! In short she looked every bit the bag lady. If anyone's plight appeared worse than her own, it was this unfortunate creature. Here she was about to take her life, and she's dickering with this poor soul over a lousy lottery ticket.

It had been such a long time that she had almost forgotten what it was like to feel compassion for another person. She forgot how to give it when she felt that she was no longer receiving it. Now this wretched soul was plea bargaining with her for a little bit of it. That's what this was really all about, wasn't it? If she would be compassionate enough to give a nobody something for nothing. It had truly been a long time since she had done anything like that. The apple was nothing. Meant nothing. Or did it?

Tired of waiting, the bag lady made a final offer. "I promise you that if you're willing to trade me that ticket for this apple, you'll discover the secret."

For the first time in so long that she couldn't remember, Marybeth freely chose to get taken. She handed over the lottery ticket for the Heart of Christ. The bag lady took it and ran.

"I might as well eat it," she said to herself as she sat down again. "The condemned man ate a hearty meal." She didn't care about where it came from or who gave it to her or how dirty it might be. Somehow it didn't matter any more. And, truth to tell—she was just a little bit curious. She bit into the apple.

It was delicious. Not incredibly delicious. Not magically delicious. Just sweet and good the way apples are. But, it made her cry. Cry for the common, ordinary, everyday goodness she had been missing. Cry over all the wasted years. Cry about all the truly meaningless arguments. Cry over the selfishness and bitterness and unforgiveness. She cried a flood of tears over all that was lost. It was the loss that got to her. Husband, children, job, happiness. She thought of Jim and how much she still loved him despite the hurts and disappointments. Were they deliberate or simply a reaction to her? She had never thought of it before. Hadn't Carol and Mark gone away to school because she had gone away to work? When did she stop seeking a middle ground? It had even cost her her job.

What was the Heart of Christ this apple symbolized? Sweetness, the way the apple was sweet? No. The apple was ordinary. Sweet but ordinary. She thought about the bag lady. In the end she felt sorry for her. Maybe it was because she identified with her—down and out. Yet, they were both willing to dicker. That must mean that there was still some hope. A moment's compassion had led her to hope. Could that be the secret?

She sat there until the sun started to go down. But, no longer on her life. There was just enough spark left in her to want to know if she could still make a difference. Finding that wallet and confronting the bag lady had given her enough pause to reconsider her decision. At least, for the time being. She left the bench and went home. As for the secret, she knew, of course, that there was no secret.

Years later she and her husband were once again deeply in love with each other, her children were close and affectionate almost to the point of distraction, and life had become truly sweet. There was only one nagging need left in Marybeth's life. She had to do something to give back what she had gained on that fateful Autumn afternoon. So she took one of her husband's old wallets and tore it apart. She went to the Salvation Army Center for some used clothes. She smeared her face and hands with dirt, but not so much so that it would be obvious. She wrapped an apple in cellophane. Then she bought a lottery ticket and headed for Belvista Lookout.

"That's mine!" she yelled.

She knew the minute he picked up the wallet that she had him. You see, at that point, she finally learned the bag lady's secret. There really was one after all. It was rather simple when you stopped to think about it. The secret was—If you pick up the wallet, there is still hope.

The truly spiritual man is not afraid of death, because he is already dead. Death would simply be redundant.

SUNDAY MORNING

*I*t was Sunday morning, and I awoke feeling rested and refreshed. The sun was already well into its course in the eastern sky, but the earth seemed so vibrant and alive that the birds just kept right on singing, if no longer to greet the sunrise then in morning praise. I put on some comfortable clothes and decided to go walking. Because it was Sunday, I read some scripture before leaving so that I might have something to reflect on while I was walking.

It was a glorious day. Every color was a feast for the eyes. The emerald fields, the ruby, gold, and lavender flowers, the bronze earth and sapphire sky were far more spectacular than any plagiarized copy on an artist's canvas. The song of the birds, the chirping of insects, and the rustle of the breeze through the trees were a symphony greater than any by Beethoven or Bach, or any chorale by Handel or Wagner. All these filled my heart and lifted my spirit. My cup ranneth over.

Then, quite suddenly, my meditation was shattered by a sharp commanding voice. Some gentleman dressed in his Sunday finest and toting the Bible shouted out at me, "Go to church!" as he ushered his family into their station wagon.

A crimson tide of embarrassment washed over me. I had been caught—like a child passing a note in school, like a thief with his hand in the till, like a swimmer with his pants down, like a boy playing hooky. I had been found out.

Then, just as quickly, I thought, "Hold on! Who do you think you are, you pious hypocrite? Here you are marshaling your family off to a church built by human hands while I am worshiping in a cathedral built by God. And how dare you judge me, you judgmental Pharisee! Is not my worship out here just as good if not better than your distracted prayers indoors? Who do you think you are anyway?"

All these things I thought, but instead I called back in retaliation, "I am in church!" Good comeback. Let him stew over that. But, in that instant my good spirit fled and my cup leaketh out. I walked past him and thought: If you have anything to say now, talk to my behind!

The remark had an effect. The gentleman stopped just short of entering the car. The earth became deathly quiet as if waiting in hushed silence for the battle to be joined. The hairs on the back of my neck bristled in anticipation.

At last it came. "Hey, you! Wait a minute!"

I turned and with clenched teeth faced him.

"Would you pray for me?" he said. "I think I need it more than you do."

———

In the end it is not arguments and rational proofs that lead one to God. It is example!

———

THE MAD HATTER'S OTHER TEA PARTY

"*D*o come in," said the Mad Hatter. "Welcome to my tea party. Only the loveliest people can attend. You'll find that everyone and everything here is so very lovely and agreeable, as every tea party should be, I'm sure you'll agree."

It was not a question. Simply a rhetorical comment. In any event, if I wanted to comment, I couldn't have as the Mad Hatter rambled on.

"No stuff and nonsense here. No one coarse or boorish. That's not allowed. No. No. Definitely not allowed. Everything simply perfect. Everyone positively lovely. All things as they should be. Nothing out of place. Not a single thing that doesn't belong. Never a 'no never mind.' Never a nose out of joint. All i's dotted. All t's crossed, as you can see."

I was so totally preoccupied with the Mad Hatter and his ongoing monologue that I had taken no notice of the other guests at table. Had I been given the opportunity to, I would have seen that as soon as he made that last comment, each of them took out a sheet of paper and started dotting i's and crossing t's.

"Everything agreeable. Everyone agreeable. Don't you agree?"

This time the guests did respond. "We agree. We agree. We agree. We agree. We agree."

I might have, simply because everyone else did, and I didn't want to appear disagreeable, but the Mad Hatter didn't wait for me. He droned on.

"Won't do. Won't do. It simply won't do," he exclaimed.

"What won't?" I asked, never thinking I'd be able to get a word in edgewise. I got the word in, but I needn't have bothered. He went on anyway.

"It won't do for you to attend my party without a boutonniere. Tea parties are always formal, you see, and everyone must always be presentable. A carnation just like mine and you will look perfect." He reached into a bowl of large chrysanthemums, broke off a white one like his, and pinned it on my lapel—right side. It was far too big and it looked foolish. Besides, it wasn't a carnation.

"Excuse me!" I shouted in a vain attempt to interrupt him.

"Won't do. Won't do. It simply won't do to have anyone shout. No one shouts at a tea party. Everyone and everything must be quite lovely and agreeable. You must use your sweetest voice, you see."

In the sweetest voice I could muster, I repeated, "Excuse me." But, before I could explain that he had given me a chrysanthemum and not a carnation, the Mad Hatter rambled on.

"I can't, you see."

"Can't what?" I asked.

"Can't excuse you," he replied.

"I don't understand," I said.

"I can't excuse you until you've had some tea. It just isn't done. How would it look if I invited you to tea and excused you before you had any? What would people say? It simply isn't done."

"I didn't want to leave the party," I said. "I . . ."

"Well, now that that's been taken care of, we must get on with things, mustn't we." Again it wasn't a question, but a statement of fact. The chrysanthemum had become a lost issue.

"Bring our guest a cup of tea," he called to someone, I had no idea who since none of the guests stirred. "Lemon, no milk. Two sugar," he said.

"I prefer milk, if you don't mind," I said.

"Everything the same," he said. "And everyone agreeable." He lifted his cup for me to see. "You have to see the tea, you see, otherwise how could it be tea." Again, it was not a question but an observation of fact. The guests all agreed agreeably.

To be tea you must see tea? Hardly. They may all agree but not me. As you can see. But not he. He rambled on.

"Please be seated," he said.

I took a seat at the table facing the others, who curiously were all seated on the same side of the table.

"That simply won't do," said the Mad Hatter. "You must sit on the other side with the others. Everyone the same and everything agreeable."

The others all agreed. "We agree. We agree. We agree. We agree. We agree."

Before the Mad Hatter could utter another word I interjected. "Shouldn't that be *everything* the same and *everyone* agreeable?" I turned quickly toward the guests seated opposite me and said, "Don't you agree?"

How could they not, if everyone was to be agreeable? But, to agree with me was to disagree with the Mad Hatter. They were trapped.

Unfortunately, I was wrong. They said not a word. They simply all came and sat on my side of the table while the Mad Hatter took his place on the opposite side. I later learned this is what is called diplomacy. I decided to drink my tea.

As I reached for my cup, the others to a man all "ah-hemmed" me. Though they said not a word, I gathered they were waiting for the Mad Hatter to pick up his cup first. It must not be agreeable to start before him. I was right. When he did, they did. But when I reached for mine they "ah-hemmed" me again. What now? I wondered, careful not to question lest I appear disagreeable. The others all lifted their cups with their left hands. Being right handed, I was about to lift my cup in the usual way again when I was politely but more forcefully "ah-hemmed" again.

So as not to appear disagreeable, I switched hands. Everyone smiled. Then, when I lifted my cup for another sip, I got the usual "ah-hemm." Now what ? I thought again, rather than asking, as I was strangely being reduced to silence like the others at the table. Then, it dawned on me. They lifted their cups only when the Mad Hatter lifted his. They kept in perfect synchronization with his movements. Cup up. Cups up. Cup down. Cups down. Everyone together. Everyone agreeable.

It was finally becoming clear to me what was happening. I should have guessed when the Mad Hatter pinned the boutonniere on my right side instead of the left. I should have known when the guests all had to sit on the opposite side of the table from him. Why we all had to drink tea with our left hands. The Mad Hatter was right handed. We were all meant to be mirror images of him. Only backward—so that he alone was right.

At that moment I knew what I had to do. I looked directly at the Mad Hatter and picked up my tea cup with my *right* hand. I did not wait for him to move first. The next move was his. How agreeable would *he* be? Would he follow my lead? Could he?

He saw the challenge in my gesture. His face flushed. Then, it got redder and redder. You could almost see steam rising above his hat. Would he? Could he? In the next moment he exploded— with a sound that was curiously like the whistle of a tea kettle gone to boil.

I jumped with a start.

"Tea's on," the chairman announced to the assembled committee. "Let's all have a nice refreshing cup of tea," he said.

The board responded.

"Of course."

"Certainly."

"Most assuredly."

"My sentiments exactly."

"Delightful."

I flushed with embarrassment. I had been daydreaming. To a man they all looked at me. Everyone agreeable. Everything always the same.

"Not today," I said.

———

Moral: The ego is always the chairman of the board.

——————

Words are the platters on which the truth can be served, embellished, or skewered.

——————

GIFTMAS

THE GHOST OF CHRISTMAS FUTURE

"Merry Giftmas!" he said.

I wasn't sure what he said. "I beg your pardon."

"I said, 'Merry Giftmas'!"

"Giftmas? Do you mean Merry Christmas?"

Now it was his turn to look dumbfounded. "What do you mean Christmas?"

"I mean Christ—mas," breaking it down into syllables as if it were two words. "You know, the birthday of Christ," I said it almost facetiously.

"Christmas?" he exclaimed. "You must be from another planet. I haven't heard that in years. Not since I was a little boy." He looked at me quizzically and added, "A very little boy."

Seeing that he looked well up in years, I attributed his remark to senility so I explained almost patronizingly. "Christmas. You know—that time of year when we decorate Christmas trees, put colored lights around our homes, play carols, send cards, and exchange gifts."

"Right!" he said and I heaved a sight of relief. "Of course, we do all that—string colored lights around the house, play carols, send cards . . . ." Now he was patronizing me. "Except, we decorate *evergreen* trees and we don't exchange gifts."

I felt like I had suddenly been transported to the Twilight Zone. Who was out of touch—me or this extraterrestrial? "We'd better take this one step at a time," I said. Where to begin? "December 25 right?"

"Right."

"Christmas—right?"

"Wrong."

"Wrong? What do you mean wrong?"

"It's called Giftmas."

"Where did you get that from?"

"Where did you get Christmas from?"

I hate it when people answer a question with a question but rather than reprove I decided to indulge the Christmas spirit and oblige him. "Christmas is Christ's birthday. It's what we celebrate on December 25."

"Is that where that word came from?" He looked genuinely surprised as if it were a revelation. "I didn't know what the word meant as a child, and then I stopped hearing it altogether. Christ was some sort of religious figure wasn't he?"

I was almost floored by the remark. Some sort of religious figure? Now I knew I was in the Twilight Zone. Or was this a dream? If it was, I didn't know if people in a dream could know that they were dreaming. In any event I felt compelled to play this out.

"I guess you could say he was a religious figure, seeing that he was the son of God." Subconsciously, the remark came out almost sarcastically. He caught the innuendo and responded in kind.

"Aren't we all," he said.

Appropriately humble for the sake of the season, I tried to explain. "No. I mean the *only* son of God."

He looked at me quizzically. "And no one else? I see now why it was a religion. Like all other religions, it was in error."

God! I couldn't believe what I was hearing. But, the last thing I wanted was to get into some kind of theological debate with this strange, if not insane, man. I would have just begged off and taken my leave except I was intrigued by all this. I decided to put the ball in his court. I knew I was on solid ground. I had to know where *he* was coming from.

"Let me see. We started this by your wishing me a Merry Giftmas, if I'm not mistaken. I believe I heard you correctly. You did say Merry Giftmas didn't you?"

"Yes I did."

"What do you mean by Giftmas?"

"It's the time we get gifts."

"Hold on!" I interrupted. You told me that you don't exchange gifts." I thought I had trapped him with his own words. Hoisted on your own petard, I thought triumphantly. But I gloated prematurely.

"We *don't* exchange gifts," he said. "We get them for ourselves."

"*For yourselves?*" I shouted incredulously.

"You seem surprised." It was his turn to interrupt. "How else would you get them?"

"As presents from others." Was he putting me on? Was this all a joke?

"Why on earth would you depend upon others to give you gifts?" There was a brief silence while he seemed to muse on the possibility. Then, as if thinking out loud, he continued. "Why would anyone want to give you a gift? Why would you want someone to if you could just as well get it for yourself. It doesn't make sense."

I thought I'd better do some explaining here and get him straight on what Christmas is all about. "You've got it all wrong," I said. "Christmas is a time for giving . . . giving to others."

"Are you telling me that's the way religious people used to think? Okay, I'll play along. It sounds interesting."

This was too much. Was he playing me for a fool? Was he humoring me or should I humor him? Where do you start when it comes to explaining Christmas to an extraterrestrial?

"Christmas is the time of year when people think of others, especially loved ones, by giving them presents."

"Wait a minute!" he interrupted. "You're telling me that you give a present to someone you love and someone you love gives you one in return?"

"That's right."

"Well, that makes no sense. Why bother? Wouldn't it be easier for people to just give themselves what they want rather than going through the fiction of pretending they're getting it from somebody else?"

"That's not exactly how it works." I tried to defend myself but saw the inescapable logic of his analysis. "It's the idea of getting it from somebody else. "

"What if you don't get what you want? Does that mean that you can never get for yourself?"

"Not at all. It's just that it's better when you get it from somebody else."

"Why? Because you don't have to pay for it?"

"I suppose it sounds that way."

"Well, then, let me put it this way. If you give a present to someone you love and they don't give you one in return, it's okay."

"Well, to be honest with you, maybe once or twice but not indefinitely."

"Would they be hurt if you didn't reciprocate?"

"Probably."

"Then why would you bother? If you buy yourself what you want, you don't put expectations on anybody else, nobody's hurt and you're both happy."

This conversation was definitely not going the way I wanted. The frustrating thing was that everything he said seemed so damned logical. I felt that I had to salvage something or lose Christmas altogether. Then, I thought of it.

"Not for Santa Claus. He brought presents and expected none in return." I heaved a sigh of relief.

"Who is Santa Claus?"

He caught me off guard. I didn't expect him not to know who Santa Claus was. Or was he still putting me on? How does one explain Santa Claus? "Look, Santa Claus is a wonderful jolly old man who brings gifts to children all over the world on Christmas Eve. He does not expect anything in return."

"Why just children?"

Damn it! He did it again. This man was either insane or insanely clever. I took a while and thought very carefully before I answered. "Because adults are expected to do it for themselves. Children can't reciprocate because they don't have the money," I said.

"Now that sounds wonderful!" he cried. "How did it work?"

I finally felt like I was getting the upper hand. "The children would draw up a list of things they wanted and put it in a letter to Santa Claus."

"And he would bring them all they wanted without expecting anything in return? How remarkable!"

"Well, not exactly."

"What do you mean 'not exactly'?"

"Well, they didn't necessarily get *everything* they wanted."

"Even so, something is better than nothing. At least they got something."

Reluctantly I had to admit that that wasn't always true either. "That isn't always the case," I confessed. "It depends."

"Depends?" He looked at me distrustfully. "On what?"

"On a lot of things. Like, if the children were good that year. . . " Before I could go on he startled me by shouting out,

"Ha! Wouldn't you know? Who could possibly expect children to be good for a whole year?"

Suddenly, his whole demeanor was one of disdain. "They were right about religions. They used double talk with the people. What amazes me is how anybody with an ounce of intelligence could be taken in. You tell me there was a kindly old man who would bring gifts to children on Christmas Eve, but only if they were good all year. Did he ever leave home?"

I got angry at his outburst. "No one really expected the children to be good all year," I shot back. "It was just something you said to them to get them to behave."

"So, it was just double talk. You told them that this Santa Claus would bring them presents if they were good all year but he would bring them presents even if they weren't. Is that the idea?"

"Not if they were really bad."

"How would he know? Did the parents write and tell him?"

God. This is getting out of hand, I thought. "Look. This is getting us nowhere. Let's just change the subject."

"That, too, is what they told us religions do. When they explained it to us as children I found it hard to believe that intelligent people could act that way. Now, I see that they were right. Do you really believe what you are saying or is this just an exercise to illustrate religious thinking?"

Now I was furious. He was playing me for a fool. But, I had an ace up my sleeve and decided to play it. "You are obviously telling me that you don't believe in religions on the one hand and then you wish me Merry Giftmas on the other. Let me remind you that the *mas*," I spelled it just to make sure he knew what I was talking about, "M—A—S, stands for Mass which is a *religious* ritual." Got you, you arrogant bastard. I had lost my cool completely.

He looked at me with a sort of pathetic expression. Without shouting back and with no rancor in his voice he said, "*Mas* stands for 'more'. It's the Spanish word for it. When I said Merry Giftmas it means I wish you 'more gifts' this year than last. It has nothing to do with religion."

I was speechless. What could I say? "Is this what Christmas has evolved to?" I wondered.

And in all the confusion of this bizarre, surreal episode, if I had the ability to read his thoughts I would have heard him say, "Is that what religion evolved to?"

Instead, I let my heart speak. After all, that's where Christmas really is.

"Let's start over," I said.

Two Things

Of two things I am certain. First, that the mind of God and the heart of man are veiled. Second, that it is love alone that can penetrate the veil.

COUNTRY ROAD

"*I*t's hot!" the left brain said to the right brain as they walked along the country road. "Almost unbearably so."

"I'll wish for a breeze," the right brain replied.

"If only wishing would make it so," the left brain laughed.

"I will wish for a breeze," the right brain replied, undaunted.

"I'm waiting," the left brain cried impatiently.

"I'm wishing," the right brain answered.

"I'm waiting."

"I'm wishing."

"I'm still waiting."

"I'm still wishing."

At last there came an ever-so-gentle, little breeze. Before the right brain could say a word, the left brain blurted out, "Don't think you're responsible for that breeze. I am! I grew so impatient with your foolishness that I started walking faster. That's what created the breeze."

"I know," the right brain said. "That's what I was wishing."

THE FARM GIRL

*S*he was just a farm girl, but she had dreams, big dreams.

"Watch out for dreams," the village *strega* told her. "They may fill your head, but they can break your heart. Peasant dreams are like peasant purses . . . always empty. "

"That doesn't have to be," she said defiantly. "One can always wish for better things."

"Wishes," the old witch-mother warned, "spite you even while you make them."

"What do you mean?'

"It isn't enough that they are as empty as the air, but they take up time and in so doing they empty it of more practical occupations. "

"Well, if that's the case I needn't worry," the peasant girl replied. "I don't waste my time with wishes. I have only one— to be a wealthy woman. Then, my dreams spend the wealth during the night while others sleep."

The *strega* laughed at her quick wit. "Then, my child, you shall be a wealthy woman. That I can promise you."

The old witch-mother was prophetic. She did become a wealthy woman. She left the farm village, married, and had children. To her willingness to work hard she joined a keen mind and a jovial disposition so that she immediately began to prosper in business. Before long she lived in a castle by the sea enjoying great wealth and popularity. Her wish and her dream had become one and real.

But fate is nothing if not fickle, and in one unfortunate and hapless business venture her fortune was lost overnight. Once again she was a penniless peasant. Or so the village women said when they chided the *strega* for making her an empty promise.

"Not so!" the witch-mother retorted. "She *is* a wealthy woman. She was already a wealthy girl years ago when she came to see me. I merely said what I saw to be true. The loss of her fortune did not diminish her in the least, for her wealth did not come from her possessions. She is as rich now as she ever was." Seeing that her words had marred their jealous gloating, she added, "It is not wealth that makes a princess out of a peas-ant, which is why she is there and you are still here."

So the farm girl moved into a different castle by the same sea.

There is a difference between being unique and being special. We are already unique by the fact of our birth. The problems begin when we want to be special. God makes us unique. We make ourselves special.

BENEDICTION

*D*ong.

Dong.

Dong.

As the golden sun slowly sank in the crimson west, the vesper bell of the cathedral tower sonorously summoned the weary faithful to evening worship to pay homage to the passing day and reap the rewards of a long day's labor.

Venite.

Venite omnes.

Come. Come all. The polyphonic voices of an angelic choir repeated the invitation over and over again—at times softly alluring and sweetly urging, then at other times more demanding and strident than gently inviting.

The long procession commenced precisely as the last rays of dusk filtered through the lavishly jeweled rose window. First, twelve thurifers walking two abreast swinging smoking thuribles like pendulums in near-perfect synchronization. Billows of sweet smelling incense—jasmine, juniper, coriander, patchouli, pine, and all manner of exotic spices from the four corners of the earth trailing in their wake.

Next, in strict liturgical order, were the minor, tonsured clerics carefully aligned according to their dates of birth from the youngest to the oldest. Black cassocks, plain white surplices, hands pressed together right thumb over left.

Then came the porters, lectors, and acolytes also arranged according to seniority by age, date of investiture, and rank of diocese.

These were followed by simple priests, the youngest by ordination date to the oldest. They wore black cassocks with or without sashes and finely embroidered lace surplices.

Monsignors were next in the progression. They, too, were carefully ranked according to dates of appointment and degrees of honor bestowed upon them from Very Reverend Monsignors and Right Reverends to Prothonotaries Apostolic. They were adorned in varying degrees of red from black cassocks with red piping and red buttons to full crimson cassocks.

Abbots and Superiors of Major Religious Orders followed because there were no laymen with special ecclesiastical papal honors.

Then came the Bishops—Most Reverends, Doctors of Divinity, Successors to the Apostles—dressed in royal crimson, gold pectoral crosses, and jeweled rings.

Ecce!

Ecce!

Ecce! Sacerdos magnus.

Behold! the great priest, the heavenly host announced. The Cardinal completed the procession—so that the last on earth would be assured the first place in heaven. Caparisoned in regal purple with ermine cape, white buskins, jeweled mitre and gold crosier, and minor clerics in attendance, he trod his way to the place of honor at the head of the table.

The vesper service followed with the appropriate psalms, orations, tracts, and hymns. At long last the Cardinal made his way to the altar and genuflected before the tabernacle. The twelve thurifers with smoking thuribles knelt six abreast on either side of the altar. As the cardinal unlocked the tabernacle, the choir exploded.

Gaudete!

Gaudete!

Rejoice! The Cardinal extracted a ponderously large and ornate ciborium from the sacred receptacle and turned toward the congregation. Once again, according to strict rank from the least to the greatest, the clerics all lined up two by two and approached the sanctuary.

First, a pair of tonsured minor clerics approached with hands extended. The Cardinal reached into the cup. He then placed one coin into the hands of each cleric. The porters, lectors, and acolytes followed and each received two coins. Simple priests received three coins. Very Reverend Monsignors got four. Right Reverends and Prothonotaries Apostolic five and six respectively. Abbots got eight. Superiors of Major Religious Orders, nine. The Bishops all got ten and the Cardinal ten times ten. After each received their due they quickly processed out of the cathedral.

Gaudete!

Gaud . . .

Click.

The sacristan turned off the sound system. The cathedral was empty. In worn-out shoes and threadbare clothes he trod wearily down the center aisle of the nave and out of the cathedral's massive oak doors, locking them behind him. Slowly he made his way into the darkness and the night bound for home. Home to wife and children. Home to family . . . and benediction.

Honor is not something you wear on your body like a costume, or an epaulet you wear on your sleeve, or a medal decorating your heart. Honor cannot be bought at any price. It is not an adornment. Honor is the language of a battle-scarred soul and its idiom is valor.

LOVE

As a child with tear-filled eyes I came before the Shaman and asked:

"Isn't it love when you are smothered with hugs and covered with kisses? When you are heaped with praises for every little thing you do and excuses are made for you even when you do wrong. Doesn't love mean that you are always forgiven no matter what, and that you should never be punished? Isn't love always kind, softhearted, affirming, and indulgent? Doesn't being loving mean that you are supposed to give and give without measure, without regard to cost or feeling? Isn't it love when you never make another person cry?

"That is not love," The Shaman answered. "You are simply spoiled," he said and sent me away.

* * *

As a youth I rushed to the Shaman and breathlessly exclaimed:

"This must be love. My heart is pounding. My blood is racing through my body. My breathing is so rapid I'm about to pass out from lack of oxygen. My knees are knocking, my legs are like butter, and I have goosebumps all over. I want to laugh and dance and shout for joy all the time. Every part of my body is throbbing with excitement. I feel exhilarated, titillated, and pixilated. Tell me this is love. I can feel it down to my very bones."

"That is not love," the Shaman answered. "You are simply hyperventilating," he said and dismissed me.

* * *

As a young adult I invited the Shaman to my celebration and said:

"Now, I know I have found love. After searching far and wide, we have finally found one another. We are compatible in every way. It seems that whatever one of us is lacking the other automatically makes up for, so unhesitatingly and flawlessly that it is almost uncanny. We have the same goals, hopes, and aspirations. We understand one another other perfectly and accept each other's faults and limitations willingly. We are so complementary that it is impossible to conceive of ourselves as ever having been apart, like two sides of the same coin. Now, tell me that isn't love?"

"That is not love," the Shaman answered. "It is a business," he said and left.

* * *

When I was sick in bed with exhaustion and fever, my body racked with pain, the Shaman came to visit me.

"I am dying," I said. "I have given and given, and each giving gave me as much pain as it did pleasure. Half of my adult life I couldn't tell if what I felt was giddiness or dizziness. Even when I felt lightheaded, I wasn't sure if it felt good or if I was seasick and wanted to vomit. I can no longer remember if all the tears I shed were tears of joy or tears of sadness. My heart is mush, my knees are weak, I am always out of breath, I have welts all over, and my legs beneath me are like butter. I can't seem to do anything right anymore, and my goals have long since gone with the wind. Now I know that every joy comes with a sorrow like two sides of the same coin."

"That is love," the Shaman said and sat down to commiserate with me.

———————

Any time we discover something good we are experiencing God in virtual reality.

———————

TOYS

*T*wo boys were playing marbles. The younger was faring much better in spite of the fact that the older boy had a shiny, oversized steel shooter.

"Let me see that shooter!" he barked at the youngster, snatching the glass shooter from his hand. It was just an ordinary glass shooter with the usual swirls of color inside. It was lighter than his own and smaller, but it had somehow bested him. He had to have it.

"I'll trade you for it," he announced and led the boy into his house.

The door he opened to his toy room was like an "open Sesame" to a world of Arabian delights. There were toys there that the young boy never believed could be anywhere except in a department store.

Unfazed by the youngster's awe, the older boy began a selection process that would take him virtually through everything in the room. Every toy he picked up he discounted as either too valuable, too important, too personal, or just too much. In the end he decided on a half deflated beach ball. The young boy refused. The older boy threw him out of the house saying, "I'll never let you play with any of my toys again."

"You never let me play with them anyway," he shouted back.

By the time the older boy became an adolescent, his toy room was filled to overflowing. Then, one day, he met a girl and fell in love. In the meantime the younger boy decided that he was just about ready to trade his shooter for almost anything in the toy room. When he offered to make a trade, the older boy not only gave him the entire room of toys, he even let him keep his glass shooter.

Moral: Love changes everything.

We tend to look at friendship through a microscope. Friendship, like great art, is best viewed from perspective.

THE GIFT

I got a gift. It was just a gift—not anything spectacular or extraordinary as far as gifts go. I could think of a hundred other gifts that I would have preferred in place of it, but nobody asked me.

It was a radio. Just a plain, ordinary radio. It wasn't stereophonic, quadrophonic, or megaphonic. It was just phonic. It had no dual speakers, no shortwave bands, no weather channel, no police scanner. It didn't even have FM. Like I said, it was just a common, run-of-the-mill radio.

It wasn't even big. It was about the size of a baloney sandwich and just about as expensive. As far as I was concerned, the only thing it had going for it was that it was portable, which isn't saying much by today's standards.

To tell the truth I hardly ever used it. On the rare occasions when I take some free time I would bring my really good portable radio with me to the park and relax listening to CDs. It's what they call a "ghetto blaster" or a "boom box." Trouble was that this radio was just too big and cumbersome to really be portable. Unless you were a macho weight lifter—which I am not. So every now and then I took my ordinary radio instead.

That was when it happened. I was sitting in the park watching the ducks skim along the surface of the lake, listening to one of my favorite radio programs, when the disc jockey said my name. My mind was so preoccupied elsewhere that I almost missed it. But, he distinctly said my name. Then he gave my address. There was no mistaking it. He meant me. Then he said that I had fifteen minutes to get to a phone and call him in order to claim my prize. I couldn't believe it.

But I was a hundred miles from nowhere. I rushed to my car and took off like a bullet. I couldn't find a phone anywhere in the park. I raced to the nearest gas station and prayed that I would make it in time. The street lights were all against me. Murphy's Law was in full swing.

Fourteen and a half minutes had passed when I got through to the station. That's what the disc jockey told me when he answered the phone. I had barely thirty seconds to spare before I would have lost "the prize of a lifetime."

And to think, before I left for the park that evening I wasn't going to bring a radio along with me because I didn't feel like lugging that heavy weight through the park. It was a last minute thing to take the small portable. It was laying on the shelf in the closet when I got my jacket so I just grabbed it. Lucky thing I did.

If you're wondering what "the prize of a lifetime" was, so did I when I called in to the station. I couldn't remember. No, it wasn't a portable radio. It was twenty-five thousand dollars.

Not a great fortune as far as fortunes go, but big enough to thrill me. You see, I used it to pay for a professional education which got me a great job in which I'm doing exceedingly well.

One last thing. I left that common, ordinary portable radio in the park when I rushed out to make that call. When I went looking for it the next day I was sure it would be gone. But it was still there lying on the grass near the bushes where I left it. I know that others must have seen it because it was just off the main path to the lake. It was probably because it looked so ordinary that no one bothered to take it. I laughed out loud as I picked it up.

"You may be ordinary," I said, "but you brought me good news that changed my life."

I still have that radio. I listen to it every day. After all, it's a very special radio.

Moral: The ordinary can be used to extraordinary advantage.

SEEDS

A seed said to itself, "I am all there is. I am perfectly formed and wonderfully made. There is no more."

"Not so!" said the voice of Wisdom.

So Wisdom took some seed and planted them in the ground. But some remained closed and rotted in the earth. Those that were open burst forth into plants.

"We are all there is," said a plant. "With our sturdy stems and fine leaves, we are perfectly formed and wonderfully made. There is no more."

"Not so!" said the voice of Wisdom.

Those plants that had gone so far and would go no more died and were no more. But those plants that were open burst forth into flowers.

"We are all there is," said a flower. "With our many colors and sweet perfume, we have finally arrived. There is no more."

"Not so!" said the voice of Wisdom. Those flowers that had given themselves to beauty and aroma were cut and put in vases. They gave delight to some but not many and then were cast away. Yet the others who were open suffered from the scourge of wind and bees and insects. True, their beauty and fragrance gave delight to many, but perhaps, too many. Thus despoiled, they died. "We were all there was," they said. "There is no more."

"Not so!" said the voice of Wisdom. Their seed was carried far and wide covering the entire countryside. And when winter passed a voice was heard in the earth that said, "We believe!" and the world came alive once again.

Moral: To those who are open there is always more.

I HAD A GARDEN

I had a garden. Fit for a king, I thought. I had been cultivating it for years on years. Every part of it was carefully planned, meticulously sown, and painstakingly husbanded. There was balance with plants drawn from both native and foreign soils. There was variety from variegated flowers to numerous fruits and vegetables. No one blossom predominated, no one fruit or vegetable reigned.

I saw that it was watered regularly; fertilized periodically; sprayed intermittently, and weeded constantly. I guarded it against storms and drought, pests and foraging herbivores. When there were lapses of care they were only occasional and always quickly remedied.

I was proud of my garden.

But an enemy came and ravaged it. The flowers were uprooted, the fruits and vegetables torn asunder and laid waste. The ground was trampled underfoot and nature poured a drenching rain that flooded what little remained.

When the sun returned it baked the ground leaving it further marred with deep and dry earthenware scars. For months and months I let it lay there as fallow and lifeless as I was.

When at last I grew restless, eager for purpose and direction once again, I tilled the soil as before but this time nothing I planted would grow. Instead, the more I worked the less successful all my efforts were. Finally, frustrated and dispirited I gave up altogether.

Then, from out of nowhere a wild flower sprung up in the garden. As I had done so many times before, more out of habit than desire, I tended it just as I had always done with those I had planted. Another appeared of a different variety and in separate corner of the garden. This too I tended. Others followed in haphazard fashion, oblivious of order, without rhyme or reason. These also I accepted and tended as best I could. In time there was a whole new garden.

This garden I could take no pride in for it was Nature's own and not mine. I had merely tended what nature had provided. It was not exactly what I wanted or the way I would have wanted it, but it was beautiful nonetheless. Besides, there was one very major difference between this one and mine. This garden brought me peace.

Moral: Sometimes there's our way and sometimes there is Nature's.

THE CALL OF THE WILD

"*C*ome," said the mountain beckoning to me. "I have something to show you."

"What is it you will show me?" I asked, my soul overflowing with excitement.

"Come and you shall see."

I stood at the base of the majestic mountain in speechless awe at the wonder that towered above me. What inestimable delight awaited me? What profound mystery would the mountain reveal to me?

Though I wondered in my heart, I felt certain I knew. There would be grandeur greater than I had ever imagined. There would be wondrous vistas that would hold me breathless. There would be cascading waterfalls and swift flowing brooks, herds of meandering elk and gentle frolicking fawns. The clouds would brush against the tree tops, and the owl would ask me, "Who am I come to visit this enchanted wonderland?" And I will say, "The mountain herself has beckoned me and I have come."

So I began my ascent with anticipation in my spirit and joy in my heart. The snow fell and each flake I took to be a greeting card from heaven. The aspen and pine embraced the path on either side of me, leading me onward and upward. "I am coming," I called excitedly to the mountain and she whispered back to me, "Come. I have something to show you."

But the path twisted and wound as it climbed making my ascent slow and labored. The thick forest soon ceased to embrace me. Instead, it began to hover about me ominously. There were no vistas to see nor wonders to behold. There was no welcoming herd of deer, nor even a lowly rabbit to lend me company. Nature was withdrawing, leaving me to the cold and the encroaching darkness. As the light waned so did my spirit with it.

"When?" I called above the mounting storm.

"Soon," she replied but I barely heard for the biting cold that numbed my ears and the mounting fear that gripped my heart.

Still, I plod onward through the drifts and the blinds, the end nowhere in sight. When I came upon a promontory the vista stretching below me served only to remind me of how far I had come and how far it was to return. The falling snow that had delighted me now frightened me as it covered my tracks assuring me that I was lost. The night owl, the harbinger of darkness and death, challenged me. "Who are you to venture forth in this awesome place?"

"A fool," I cried. "Nothing more than a fool."

Through the blinding snow I could barely see the mountain top just ahead of me. Was this the prize I had been called to? Was this the feat I had been invited to? "Too late," I cried for the wind and the cold had sapped the last of my strength, and I could go no further. I gave one last desperate call to the mountain, but she did not answer me. Even if she had, I feared that I would no longer hear her. I had been betrayed.

Then, as I slumped in despair, I heard her call. She called again, and I saw her making her way toward me. Suddenly, my heart raced with excitement, and its warmth restored my spirit. It was a young Indian brave who heard my desperate cries in the wilderness and came to me. His presence restored my hope, his countenance brought me peace, and his warmth warmed me. Even though the summit was within reach, he turned me around, and I began my downward trek. I no longer looked to the right or the left nor up—only down as I followed the tracks he left. And somewhere in my descent he was gone, and I failed to even ask his name.

At the base of the mountain, I turned in anguish and sorrow to cast one last, angry glance at the mountain.

"Why?" I cried.

"Because it was what you wanted," she replied.

"What?" I raged at her. "To be deceived? Is that what I wanted?"

"I did not deceive you," she replied.

"'Come,' you said. 'I have something to show you.' I saw nothing but fear and despair. If not for that young Indian brave I would most surely have died."

"I know," she whispered. "I sent him to you."

"Then what was this all for?"

"I taught you what you needed to know."

"And what pray tell was that?" I asked cynically.

"Faith," she replied, and her voice faded with the passing wind.

THE PHOTOGRAPH

*I*t was their first date. They were young, not quite past adolescence, and the future spread before them like an open oyster.

They spent the day at Coney Island letting the different attractions cement their initial attraction for one another into what would become a permanent bond. That afternoon they took a leisurely stroll along the beach and came upon a newly built magnificent beach house. It was their "dream house." A kindly passer-by consented to take their picture as they posed in front of it.

She put the photograph in her album, relegating the negative to oblivion. The picture remained there for years, at first deluged with others commemorating births, baptisms, first steps, picnics, and parties. But, as the years passed, the photographs became fewer and fewer as they gave way to slides and then videos.

As a surprise for their twenty-fifth anniversary, the children had the Coney Island picture enlarged and framed. A bit grainy and somewhat the worse for wear, it was nonetheless a treasured keepsake. It sat in the center of the fireplace mantel during the season of grandchildren. With the first great grandchild and after her husband's death, it made its way into her bedroom where she began spending more and more of her time. Eventually, it found its way to her bedside table in the nursing home. It had become the last treasure of her long life, the sentimental pearl of great price.

After she died her daughter took the photograph and gave it a place of honor on her baby grand piano. Occasionally, her children would refer to it when reminiscing about "Gramma and Gramps," but they didn't remember them ever looking that young. When she died, it found its way into her daughter's attic. It remained lost up there for two succeeding generations until a big renovation and cleanup got underway. By then, no one knew or remembered who the happy young couple was. It was simply a quaint old photograph without any personal value. Was it of somebody's great-great-grandparents?

Or perhaps a great uncle and aunt? Were they even relatives? Since they were both into neomodern, there was no place in their lives for an ancient photograph, so it made its way to a rummage sale. It was picked up by an antique dealer who discarded the broken frame and added the picture to a collection of at least a hundred others labeled "Memorabilia."

It remained there for about two more generations. Faded and worn thin and dirty through constant perusing, it was certain to be consigned to final oblivion when a historian working on a research project chanced upon it. It was not the happy young couple or nostalgia for period clothing that drew his attention but the beach house they had posed in front of. It had been built as a retirement home for the then-governor of New York State. Only two weeks after its completion and before any official photographs were taken, it had burned to the ground because of faulty wiring. It's passing had gone unnoticed and would have remained so if not for the recent publication of the governor's memoirs. In them he reveals how he had allowed the house to be used by the first-ever delegation meeting to discuss the possibility of establishing a future United Nations.

The once sentimental photograph of a happy young couple was destined to become a treasured keepsake of peace-loving people all over the world.

Moral: Personal treasures are also the world's keepsakes.

THE SIGN

*I*n the middle of a vast and wild wilderness, there lay nestled in a hidden crevasse a crystalline pool whose waters were so pure, cool, and deep that it was said by those travelers who were fortunate enough to chance upon it that it contained miraculous curative powers. So indeed it did, as was attested to by numerous other pilgrims who had found their way to the incredible pool. However, finding it was no easy matter. There was no road or footpath anywhere for one to follow. Any attempt to make one always proved futile for the strong winds, the shifting sands, the flash floods, and the tracks of wandering herds would obliterate all signs of previous passage. Nor could one trust the tracks of any previous pilgrims even if they did remain for a while, for they very well could have been lost themselves, and to follow them offered no surety whatsoever. The only certainty was that one never came out of the wilderness the same way one entered, so how could anyone leave markers? Seekers would simply have to go it alone and hope for the best.

Such was the case until the day one very specially gifted pilgrim, worn out from his wearisome trek, fell asleep beneath an outcropping of rocks. During the night an angel appeared to him and pointed toward where the mysterious pool lay hidden. The next day, in gratitude for the celestial vision and desirous of sharing his good fortune with future travelers, he carved an arrow in the rock pointing in the direction the angel had shown him. In time he also found the pool, but like all the others before him he emerged from the wilderness a different way from how he had entered it. But he had left a sign. Somehow it would be a little easier for future pilgrims.

So it happened that others came and found the sign which somehow survived all the elements that wild nature had thrown at it. The outcropping still stood, and the arrow still pointed in the direction of the miraculous pool. The spot became a haven, a spiritual if not a physical oasis in the desert. Now that one knew the direction in which to proceed, there was time to enjoy a short respite from the rigors of travel with ease of body and mind.

Thus it was that the very next pilgrim who came to the spot and the sign desired to leave his mark on the happy place. As he was an artist, he carved a spray of flowers above the arrow. He had left his gift to the arrow-carver and the angel. The next traveler was a musician and he composed a song of gratitude on the spot and engraved it in the stone below the arrow. Each pilgrim who came left his or her mark—some very elaborate and beautiful and some a simple "x" by those who were illiterate. At the outcropping, songs were sung, meals shared, stories of travel exchanged, and more marks left on the stone.

After a while, so many had left their own personal marks on the outcropping that the arrow pointing in the direction of the miraculous pool became lost in the maze of graffiti. But all was not lost. The place itself had become a center of pilgrimage so that many who came there did not even know there was more, that it was meant to direct others beyond that place to the miraculous pool, so they never felt cheated. For them the journey simply ended there.

However, future pilgrims who sought the pool found it better to avoid that place altogether rather than remain there indefinitely trying to decipher the maze in order to find the arrow.

Moral: Everything this side of heaven is a sign pointing to God.

Some people gather candles in order to shine by their light. Others gather them in order to light up the world.

THE STORY

Once upon a time there was a plot. To be perfectly honest with you, it wasn't much of a plot. Not that it was a bad plot, mind you. It's just that it wasn't all together yet. Something was missing.

So plot went to a writer and asked, "What's wrong with me?"

"Forgive me for coming right to the point and being blunt," the writer said, "But, the way I look at things—not that that's the way everyone looks at things, although I think that might not be altogether unpleasant, I mean if everyone looked at things the way I did, there certainly wouldn't be the problems that there are in the world since everyone knows that disagreements come from diverse opinions, and without differing opinions everyone would agree and that would mean they would agree with me and that's exactly the way I'd like things to be."

"But what about me?" asked the plot.

"You!" exclaimed the writer. "Haven't you been listening? Do I have to spell it out for you? You lack words. W-O-R-D-S! Why it's as plain as the nose on your face. Well, that's not altogether correct since you have no nose on your face. To be perfectly honest with you, you have no face, either. To come right to the point, you're invisible. That's your problem."

"Where I do get words from?" plot asked hoping for a simple answer. Her wish was granted. Well, somewhat.

"From a dictionary, silly. Everyone knows that you get words from a dictionary. But not just any dictionary. Don't go looking into those supermarket specials unless you want to spend the rest of your life as a virtual illiterate. *Webster's Encyclopedic Unabridged Dictionary of the English Language* is the only one for me. However, you may find…"

Before the writer could finish plot hurried off to find a dictionary.

"I need words so that I won't be invisible," she said to the dictionary.

"I have words," the dictionary said. "Plenty of words. How's this one—'grallatorial'? I like the sound of that one. Or 'metacinibar.' As you might imagine, I'm rather partial to large words. Monosyllabic words are plebeian, don't you think? I had a passion for 'antidisestablishmentarianism' until it was overused, and I might add only as a word, never in its proper context. You see words separate the classes. The more class you have, the less people understand the words you use."

"You mean to say," said plot, "if you're really intelligent you use words that no one will understand."

"Precisely!" said the dictionary.

"Isn't that an oxymoron?" plot said.

"Don't get uppity with me," the dictionary said, right out of its section on acceptable slang. "I detest those who put on airs."

"Airs is all I have to put on," said plot wistfully. "I'm invisible. You've given me words, but where do I go from here?"

"To a grammarian, a specialist in the study of grammar. A person who claims to establish or is reputed to have established standards of usage in a language."

Plot found a grammarian in his study. Seeing how busy he looked, plot asked sheepishly, "Can I have a moment of your time?"

"May I. The proper form is 'May I?' not 'Can I?' You can take it without my wanting it. My granting it requires a 'May I?'"

"I don't understand," said plot.

"I'm not surprised. So few do. It went the way of verbs in subjunctive clauses. People say, 'If I was a rich man' instead of 'If I were a rich man.' Now, inclusive language is making babbling idiots of even rhetoricians. Authors use bad grammar and call it style. What is this world coming to?" There was a momentary pause after which the grammarian exclaimed, "Oh dear me! Now, they have me doing it. To what is this world coming? To what is this world coming?"

The grammarian was so upset over his slip that plot knew it would be hopeless (or useless?) to pursue the conversation any further. Besides, she wasn't sure if she would be able to talk with him in the proper form. But he had left her with a clue. He said "author." She would seek out an author.

"What's wrong with me?" she asked.

"Nothing," he said to her delight. "You just need a little beefing up. First of all, you can't just make an appearance without being announced. It just isn't done. You need a proper introduction. But you can't show everything you've got up front right away. There's got to be some mystery. That's what makes you interesting and perhaps desirable. I say 'perhaps' because that will be determined by your body. With just the right curves and bends you will develop into a real beauty. And last but not least, you've got to leave them with a good impression. Yes, definitely! You have to give them a good impression coming and going."

Thus, the author worked with the plot long and intimately. In the end they gave birth to a story, the publisher made money, and they all lived happily ever after.

Except the grammarian, who insisted that they should all live happily ever afterwards.

Philosophers have defined man as *Homo risibilis*—capable of laughter. Where so-called prophets and saviors have failed is in their loss of humor.

Language doesn't offend God. Sins do.

THE LEPER

As he entered a village, ten lepers approached him. Keeping their distance, they called out, saying, "Jesus, Master, have mercy on us!" When he saw them, he said to them, "Go and show yourselves to the priests." And as they went, they were made clean. Then one of them, when he saw that he was healed, turned back, praising God with a loud voice. He prostrated himself at Jesus' feet and thanked him. And he was a Samaritan. Then Jesus asked, "Were not ten made clean? But the other nine, where are they?

Lk 17:12–17

* * *

Leprosy was the dreaded disease of the Bible. Among a nomadic, close knit community the fear of contagion was constant cause for anxiety. Therefore, lepers were required by custom and law to remain apart from all others and to signify their presence by crying out, "*Tame*!" "Unclean!"

Talmudic tradition

* * *

leprosy—In the New Testament, as in the Old Testament, leprosy may (also) designate a *wide variety of mild skin infections.*
Dictionary of the Bible
(Milwaukee: Bruce, 1965)

*J*onathan, the baker's son, was in love with Rebekah, the miller's daughter. In this he had a rival, Eliphaz, the cloth merchant. While Jonathan was young and strong, he was only an apprentice, and his family was dirt poor. Eliphaz, on the other hand, was considerably older, having survived two wives, wealthy, and a man of status within the community. But he was also an irascible and jealous man. When he saw that the fair Rebekah was put off by all his advances, he vowed vengeance against the unsuspecting Jonathan.

"I have reason to believe that the baker's son is a leper," he whispered to the husband of the village gossip, whose eyes widened with fear.

"If this is so, imagine the danger," he cried. "Why, all who eat his bread could be afflicted. Our whole village could be in danger."

"Oh, it is so. Of this I am sure," the merchant continued. "You see I saw him bathing at the wadi, and there on his shoulder I noticed it. The blemish. He quickly covered himself the moment he saw me. If it were not leprosy, why would he behave so?"

"Then he must immediately show himself to the priests. If we don't nip this in the bud, our whole village can end up quarantined." The man hurried off to tell his wife the news.

Eliphaz in turn went to Eleazar the priest and put enough fear of the Lord in him that he would have declared a pimple the plague. When Jonathan was driven to his door, followed by a committee of elders, the panic-stricken man declared him unclean without even a cursory examination. The hapless apprentice's fate was sealed. In spite of his protests that the blemish was merely an ugly birthmark he had kept hidden since his youth, he was exiled from the village. Even his poor father had no choice but to close up his shop and seek work in the fields.

Thus Jonathan was forced to join the leper community or forfeit his life. Charity was sparse indeed in such a small-minded community, so he eventually made his way to the outskirts of Jerusalem. There he lived for years as an outcast surviving on whatever food he and the others could gather, beg, or occasionally steal. Time and again he had appealed to the local priests, but the stigma had traveled with him, and the mere sight of the discolored skin had sealed his fate.

If life in those days was incredibly hard for the poor, it was doubly so for the sick and ostracized. For Jonathan the burden was unbearable. Although he was forced to keep his distance from those who were healthy, he refused to yield to the lie by calling himself unclean. This would then result in name calling and stone throwing until he was driven to make his way to another village where a similar fate awaited him. After a while, he ceased altogether proclaiming his innocence. Nor did he appeal any more to God who, along with the others, had dealt with him as unclean and outcast.

Then one day, while he was traveling with a band of lepers, they came upon an itinerant rabbi whom people were flocking to because he was considered a miracle worker and a prophet. Jonathan took no more interest in this Jesus from Nazareth than he would have in Elisha, who healed Naaman the Syrian of his leprosy. Why should he? He had no leprosy to be cured. Despite his protestations, the others made their way through the throng, which angrily but readily stepped aside to give them access to the preacher. Once they made their request, the great man casually sent them off with the customary, "Go show yourself to the priest."

"Fat lot of good that did you," Jonathan sneered. "Why would God heal you when it was God who afflicted you in the first place? Don't look to God for salvation. Our salvation will come from our own resourcefulness."

"That may be true for you," said Shemer the Samaritan, "since you are not yet as weak and disfigured as we are. If our salvation is not to come from God, then it must come from the generosity of those who take pity on us. Our hope is either in the charity of men or the forgiveness of God."

"I have done nothing to be forgiven for," Jonathan protested.

"Then for your father's sin."

"The sin is neither mine nor his. The sin is this stiff-necked people's who listen to malicious gossip, this bastard off-spring that will not let me work for my bread. So I am forced to take what they give me. But I will not beg. Nor will I plead for what I am willing and able to work for."

"And if they do not give it, then what?" It was the Nazarene who had quietly slipped into their midst.

"Then, by God, I'll take it."

"If you take it, it will not be by God, my friend."

"Why not, when God himself put this curse on me?"

"Shall we receive the good at the hand of God, and not receive the bad?"

"Don't quote scripture at me! It no longer applies. If you know your scripture then you know that outcasts are outside the law."

"I wasn't quoting the law, but Job. You will recall that Job was an innocent man."

"Especially Job! Unless you can assure me that in the end I, too, will be given considerably more than when I started."

"I told you, did I not? Go show yourself to the priest." The Nazarene walked off, leaving a confounded Jonathan in his wake.

But Jonathan did not do as Jesus urged. He was no leper. Besides, he already knew how the priests would react to his birthmark. The other lepers, however, did as Jesus ordered and left Jonathan standing by himself. Hours later, Shemer came rushing back.

"I'm healed," he cried jubilantly. "The leprosy is gone. The priest declared me clean."

Jonathan, taken by surprise, didn't know how to react. He wanted to stop up his ears against this unaccustomed explosion of joy and excitement. He wanted to throttle Shemer and get him to stop babbling. He wanted to hear about what happened and yet he didn't. But, in fact, he was too dumbfounded to react. Besides, he wasn't altogether happy about the Samaritan's good fortune. Shemer's good luck only served to heighten his own bad luck. The mere idea of Shemer returning to his family and village while he remained an outcast was more than he could bear. He was almost jealous of Shemer's leprosy. At least Shemer had something he could be cured of. Jonathan had something that others had to be cured of. Was there a miracle for that?

"I must thank him. I must thank the Nazarene," was all Shemer could say as he hurried on.

Jonathan felt that the irony was just too much. A Nazarene whom people looked down upon as the lowest of the low ("What good can come from Nazareth?") healing a Samaritan, a heretic half-breed, over a Jew, who can't be cured of a disease he doesn't have. It was enough the make a sane man crazy and a crazy man laugh. "Go show yourself to the priest," Jesus said. Why? So he, too, can have a good laugh?

Bitter and angry, Jonathan made his way toward Jerusalem where throngs of Jews from all over the world were streaming in for the celebration of Passover and the pickings would be good one way or another. Outside the lepers' camp, for he never fully joined in with them, he bedded down for the night. The next day was the first day of the feast and he was sure to do well if he ventured forth early enough.

Just before dawn he made his way to a nearby stream to wash. When the first full rays of sunlight streamed across his half-naked body, Jonathan saw that the ugly birthmark that marred his shoulder since birth was gone. He stared in disbelief at his clear, unblemished skin. It was completely gone, without even so much as a trace. It had somehow, miraculously disappeared, and Jonathan knew without hesitation what he would do. He had dreamt of it often enough during the early days of his exile, but the long, intervening years had eroded the memory. Now, it returned almost as quickly as the birthmark had disappeared. Defiantly, he went to show himself to the priests to be declared clean so that he could take his place in society once again. Reluctantly, he made the required sin-offering but vowed that pigs would fly before he would ever again give the priests so much as a farthing.

Jerusalem was crowded beyond capacity and endurance because of Passover so there was plenty of work for a strong and able-bodied man like Jonathan. He had eight days to accumulate a small nest egg which he planned to bring home to his father so that they could start all over again. Perhaps, another bakery. Definitely in a different village. But not before he fulfilled his dream. Definitely not until then.

He worked like a driven man, day and night without rest or sleep. There had been too much time lost and so much to make up for. Passover offered a rich harvest of work, but there were few spare laborers to do it all so merchants and tradesmen were extra generous for whatever help they could get. In only a week's time, Jonathan had fared better than he had ever managed in all his days at home.

One week after the festival, armed with a full purse and a full heart, Jonathan followed in the wake of the pilgrims who had recently vacated the city. Only because it was the custom, he took the trade route to Galilee along the Jordan, thereby avoiding ritual uncleanness by passing through Samaria. On his way from Jerusalem to Jericho he fell prey to thieves who beat and robbed him of all his money, leaving him half dead beside the road. When he awoke the next morning stripped of his clothes, his naked body covered with discolored bruises and looking much like a dying leper, he was carefully avoided and sidestepped by all who ventured by. Too weak to speak and too disheartened to care about what happened to him, he wept bitter tears. The scorching sun burned away even his will to live, when a stranger came along and lifted him onto his donkey. In the process he fainted.

He awoke to find himself in an inn. The innkeeper explained that a generous pilgrim had left him there and provided for his keep until he should return. Jonathan remained only for a short time as he was anxious to continue his journey home.

On the morning of his departure, the stranger returned. Jonathan was amazed to discover that his generous benefactor was none other than Shemer the Samaritan. For the first time since he could remember, Jonathan was happy to see someone.

"How can I repay you for your kindness? I thought I would surely die out there on the road with everyone passing me by. How did you recognize me through all the dirt and blood?"

Shemer acted just as surprised as Jonathan. "I had no idea it was you, my friend. I saw only a man in need."

"If that is so, why would you help me—a Jew—if you did not recognize me?"

"A Jew . . . and a leper," Shemer added.

"I am no leper," Jonathan shouted. But before he could explain further, Shemer cut him off, saying, "So then the Nazarene healed you, too."

"He did not!" Jonathan was almost in a rage. "I had no leprosy to begin with. Only a birthmark on my shoulder. A blemish that has been a curse all my life."

Shemer looked where Jonathan pointed. "And where is the birthmark now?" There was an eerie calmness, a kind of quiet self-assurance in the way Shemer asked the question.

"It's disappeared. Gone to hell where it belongs and I am free of its curse."

"Was it not Jesus who told the group of us to show ourselves to the priests? That we had been made clean?"

"But I had no leprosy."

Jonathan weakened only slightly, but by his tone Shemer saw that he was wavering. "Then you were made clean of the offending birthmark. Now that both our curses have been lifted, what will you do?"

Jonathan did not hesitate to reply. "I will return to my village and seek vengeance on the man responsible for all the evil that has befallen me. He has no protection against me now that I can enter the village once again. Now that I am no longer unclean."

"No longer unclean, but not yet clean," Shemer sighed.

"What are you saying? My body is clean. There is no longer a blemish on it."

"I fear that the blemish has moved within and tainted your soul. Leave vengeance to the Lord. You cannot walk through dung without stinking up yourself. Leave it to the Lord."

"Don't make me laugh!" Jonathan screamed. "Where was the Lord when this injustice was laid upon me? Where was the Lord while I suffered and my enemy prospered? "

"He was weeping over your suffering."

"Let Him keep His tears! Tears never healed a broken body."

"Do not fear those that can harm the body. Rather fear whatever can harm the soul. Tears, my friend, are the soul's anointing and the assurance of God's forgiveness."

"I have done nothing to be forgiven of." He had no sooner said this when he thought of the fat Eliphaz sitting smugly in his shop. "At least, not yet."

"Come with me, my friend, to Jesus the Nazarene," Shemer pleaded. "Listen to his sweet words and gentle wisdom. Learn as I did that there is no force on earth greater than love and no healing stronger than forgiveness. Were it not for him I would still be a leper. Were it not for his teaching, you might have died by the side of the road for before he touched my heart I hated all Jews as much as I hated leprosy."

"It is easy enough for a man to speak sweetly when the wood is green. What will he do when the wood is dry?" Jonathan retorted.

"The prophet teaches that he will respond the same way if he has prepared his heart beforehand."

"So he's a prophet too, is he? Well, let me tell you, my friend,"—mocking the way Shemer had referred to him—"that I've seen many a prophet curse God at the hands of the Romans, and the Jews as well. There is no better cure for hypocrisy than pain. Your prophet had better pray that he's not put to the test."

"It is something he has taught us all to pray for."

"Then he is at least more honest than most. Still, I'm grateful to you for having saved my life, and I'll do whatever I can within my power to repay you."

"Forgive the cloth merchant," was Shemer's remarkable reply.

Jonathan was so taken aback by the request that he couldn't believe his ears.

"Just like that?" he said.

"Just like that."

"You must be insane. The leprosy must have affected your brain. For years Eliphaz was safe and smug because I could not enter the village. Now that I am clean, he has no protection against me. It is something I have dreamed of all these long, bitter years. The thought of destroying him was at times the only thing that sustained me. And you're asking me to forget it. You can't seriously expect me to forgive him! I promised you that I would do all in my power to repay you but that is not within my power. No power on earth can stop me."

"No power on earth would want to. I am speaking of a higher power."

"If there is any prayer left in me, let alone a belief in God, it is that just as he did nothing to stop my misfortune, he does nothing to stop my good fortune."

Saddened by Jonathan's intransigence, Shemer paid the innkeeper what remained of the bill and returned home to Samaria. Jonathan hurried off to Galilee to seek his vengeance.

* * *

But fortune was not with him. Not only had the wicked Eliphaz prospered and moved on to even better things in Jerusalem, he had also succeeded in marrying the only love of his life, the fair Rebekah. The final blow however, came when he discovered that his father had died in an accident while working in the fields. What did a baker know of field work? For this, too, he held Eliphaz responsible. Anger, bitterness, and frustration ate away at his heart. He resolved to work his way back to Jerusalem where at last he would have his reckoning with Eliphaz. It was all he had left to live for.

Unfortunately, there was neither a big feast nor great commerce in Galilee to abet his plan, so it took Jonathan almost a year to gather enough money to make the journey. This time he took the direct route through Samaria. Everywhere he went it seemed that the Nazarene had preceded him. To hear of his exploits was unavoidable. Everything the man said and did was matter for discussion. While Jonathan admitted to being intrigued by what he heard he was not convinced. He didn't dare allow it until he settled the score with Eliphaz.

When he arrived in Jerusalem, the city was once again in a state of frenzy over the feast of Passover. Chaos was the order of the day with shop keepers haggling about prices, hucksters barking their wares, cart peddlers shouting at pedestrians to stand aside, parents scolding errant children, and animals bleating, braying, and barking everywhere. It would not be easy for Jonathan to learn the whereabouts of Eliphaz's shop, but no amount of confusion or delay could dampen his resolve. How in the midst of all of this he could run into Shemer again was either a twist of irony or a matter of destiny.

The Samaritan was so casual about the encounter that it seemed like they had parted only moments ago. "They have arrested Jesus," he said without so much as a greeting.

Jonathan responded similarly. "Whatever for?"

"The gossip is blasphemy. It is because he has repeatedly spoken against the Temple and the priests."

"Then he is more a prophet than I gave him credit for," Jonathan chuckled.

"Now, they are seeking vengeance against him."

The word struck Jonathan to the core. Vengeance was his daily bread so he knew that like him nothing would stop them. The Nazarene was doomed. When he didn't respond, Shemer continued.

"He is innocent. They have found scoundrels willing to lie and make false charges against him. I have seen how these priests and lawyers work. They will twist and manipulate all that he says and make it appear like a confession. Then they will kill him."

Jonathan could sympathize with the Nazarene since he had suffered the same fate. Had not a lie begun his downfall? Had not gossip twisted a simple birthmark into leprosy? Did he not die when he was cast out, doomed forever to live among the unclean? For the first time in memory, another emotion was able to edge out his anger. He felt compassion. But was it for the Nazarene or for himself?

"Make way!" someone shouted. "Make way!"

Some Roman soldiers were coming through, pushing the milling people aside with their long lances. "Get out of the way!"

Jonathan and Shemer were shoved along with some others into a shop entrance as a procession of soldiers muscled its way through the crowd. It was a cohort leading prisoners off to execution. Because of the growing numbers of pushing and shoving people, there would have been no way for them to see who the prisoners were had not one of them fallen down just in front of where they were standing. When some of the crowd made out to help him, the soldiers cruelly pushed them aside, giving Jonathan and Shemer a clear line of vision at the prisoner.

"My God, it's Jesus!" Shemer cried.

From behind them came a voice saying, "He's getting what he deserves." The voice was hauntingly familiar. In a flash Jonathan recognized it.

"My God, it's Eliphaz!" he cried.

* * *

The crowd seemed to have a will of its own as it moved like a giant wave carrying all the flotsam and jetsam along with it. Jonathan could no more move against the flow than he could swim against the tide. He looked back over his shoulder and burned into his memory the face of Eliphaz standing there and the location of his shop. He would return.

The tide deposited them all at Golgotha, where Jesus was already hanging from a cross. There was so much confusion and yelling that Jonathan could not tell if the crowd was for him or against him. Mixed—as far as he could tell. The soldiers had all that they could do to keep the different factions from attacking one another. Still, periodic fighting broke out.

Shemer had been swept away in the flood, and Jonathan found himself standing alone among the jeerers.

"Come down, prophet!" Laughter.

"Work one of your miracles now." More laughter.

"Better yet," someone near Jonathan yelled. "Tell us again how much you love us."

Rage welled up from deep within his soul. Suddenly, he saw himself standing among all the countless, faceless tormentors he had encountered over the years. All those who called names and hurled epithets at him, all those who cursed him as being accursed of God, all those who passed him by without pity or compassion, all the self-righteous who spat at him. He was standing in their midst. And Jesus on the cross had become him!

When the taunter spat at Jesus, it was too much to bear. Jonathan swung a mighty blow at the unsuspecting man and caught him full on the face. Before the hapless man could recover, he was on him like a crazed animal. Soldiers came and tore them apart. They would have arrested them both except that another skirmish broke out in the crowd and they hurried off. The fight might have resumed, but someone shouted out that Jesus was speaking, and they all wanted to hear what he had to say.

Deep down in his heart Jonathan wished that Jesus really was a miracle worker and that he could call down fire from heaven on his enemies the way Elijah did on Mount Carmel.

It was as if Jesus read his mind, for in the next moment he called out, "Eli! Eli!"

"He's calling Elijah," someone in the crowd shouted.

Jonathan felt a chill run up his spine. My God, he thought, he's reading my mind. He's going to do it. He's calling on Elijah to help him do it. Good. To hell with them. To hell with all of them. But, what would that say about his being a prophet?

What about vengeance being God's and all that? Well, like he said before, pain has done in more than one prophet. And who could blame this Jesus for losing it when crucifixion was the worst of all punishments? Go ahead. Give it to 'em, Jesus!

Jesus seemed to be looking right at him. He was convinced that he was reading his mind. Here it comes, he thought and braced himself for a shower of fire. Or, at least, fiery curses.

"Father forgive them for they know not what they do."

That's it? That's all? Forgive them . . . just like that? Jonathan thought disbelievingly.

"Just like that," Shemer said suddenly standing at his side. "I told you he was a prophet."

"Only time will tell if he was a prophet or a fool," Jonathan sighed. "But, I'll say this for him. He's one hell of a man."

"Not so." Shemer shook his head. "He's heaven's man."

* * *

When Jonathan returned to Eliphaz's shop, the fervor of his wrath had almost completely dissipated. Even as he stood outside he could hear the viperous tongue of Rebekah his wife spitting out invective after invective at him and proclaiming loudly to all the neighborhood, if not the world, what a lazy, good-for-nothing, unworthy lout of a husband she had had the misfortune of marrying. It took no great insight to see that the once proud and mighty merchant had been cuckolded by a shrew—one whom he himself might have married . . . but for the grace of God. Scripture was right. Vengeance is better left to God.

Jonathan accompanied Shemer to Samaria where he spent the rest of his life helping lepers and outcasts. And it was said among those who knew him that never was there a more single-hearted man.

Nor, one might add, a happier one.

VICTIMS

Once upon a time in the Spirit Land of God and the angels, God decided that He would create an "out there."

"Once you do that, everything out there would be separated from everything in here," the Archangel Gabriel said.

"Yes," God replied, "the way you and the angels are out there from my 'in here.'"

"True but if they are things and not spirits like ourselves, then they would be twice removed from you, would they not?"

"Not so. You forget, Gabriel, that you are not the same kind of spirit as I. You are created spirit while I am uncreated spirit. The other beings I create will be bodied spirits. You are created spirits, and they will be embodied spirits. They will dwell in me and I in them the way I dwell in you and you in me."

"And should they fail as did some of our number, how will you deal with them?"

"The same way I did with you. I will not meddle in their affairs any more than I do in yours. My spirit and power will be in them as it is in you, and that is enough for all of you. How you use it is yours to decide. The door to my heart is always open. It will be for them as it is for you—the way back."

Because of his superior mind and great perspicacity, Gabriel saw the fall of man and the terrible injustices that would follow from it in a way that could not happen with the angels. "Will you not intervene for the helpless and the innocent?" he asked.

"If I intervene in the cause of one, I must intervene in the cause of all. My grace is sufficient for the world. My power in them can overcome any and all evil."

"But what of the victims?"

"That, my dear Gabriel, will be their ready doorway to my heart."

WHY

*I*t was quiet time. The gentle evening breeze soothed them as they lay scattered beneath the barren rocks of the desert. They were all exhausted from the last onslaught of sick people who had come to him for healing. This last crowd had been especially unruly—shouting, pushing, pawing, cursing, and even fighting with one another to get to him. It was as if they were worried that his healing powers might suddenly be spent and there would be nothing left by the time they got to him. Jesus took it all in stride.

If it had been up to him, Peter thought, he would have put his foot to many a behind and sent them packing like dogs the way they deserved. They obviously could not have been listening to what Jesus was saying for them to have acted the way they did. James had taken no nonsense from the mob. He knew how to keep them in line. For him it was an exercise for the conflict to come, and this was merely strengthening him for it. Thomas, as usual, sat off by himself wondering how all of this could be and what it all meant. Judas worried about how little money was left in their paltry treasury. Why couldn't Jesus multiply that the way he did the loaves so that he wouldn't have to fret so much about where their next meal was coming from? But, on second thought, maybe this was the way he would do it. Andrew longed to go fishing again. It wasn't nearly as draining as catching men.

John, the youngest and the most naïve, ambled over to Jesus and sat down beside him. He said nothing, but his face betrayed him. He was deeply troubled.

"What's bothering you?" Jesus asked.

She was just a woman in the crowd, another face among so many nameless faces. But her body told the story. She was beyond healing, beyond hope. Others had carried her there from as far away as Bersabe, they told him, but she showed absolutely no interest in all that was going on. She bore the countenance of those who are hopelessly lost. Death was knocking at her door.

He had tried to get a response from her, but it was useless. All his talking and explaining and encouraging fell on deaf ears. He saw it in her eyes. She looked through him and beyond.

When he slumped to the ground next to her prostrate body in tears over his futile efforts, she at last turned to speak to him.

"Why?" It was all she said and then turned to face the wilderness once again. One word and nothing more. There was no need to say anything more. It was enough. That single word conveyed one and ten thousand thoughts, which all coalesced into two tears, one from each eye, that slowly etched their way down her cheeks and then lingered for an endless moment before finally falling to the parched desert earth waiting expectantly for them. At that moment she died.

John could not find the words to speak to Jesus, or tell him about his sad encounter with the dying woman and his burning helplessness in the face of such suffering and death. Instead, he just cried.

They stayed there two more days recouping their strength. By this time the last of the crowd had gone, and they were ready to make their way back. Back to another place and another crowd. Peter steeled himself for what lay ahead. James was like a restless stallion waiting to be set loose again. Thomas looked like he had resolved his last dilemmas. Judas glanced in his purse and counted what was left one last time. And Andrew hoped that their next stop would be alongside a lake.

John knew that he was leaving a piece of his heart here in the desert. He had not told Jesus about the woman because by the time he felt up to it, it was already too late, and there were so many other things to be done and people waiting to be taken care of that he just let it slip. As the group of them started out, Jesus fell behind to where John moped along. Then, without saying a word, he took his hand like a child and led him a short distance off the path.

They stopped at the very spot where the sick woman had died. Jesus raised his arm and pointed to it. John did not understand. Was this his way of showing him that he knew about the unfortunate woman? He was not surprised. But, why then hadn't he done something for her? The question froze on his lips when he looked at the spot one last time. There, on the dry and barren desert floor, two tiny white blossoms had bloomed.

BLESSED MOTHER

"Sir!" she cried, trying to make her way through the mob of followers who constantly surrounded him. "Please."

If he heard her, he didn't show it. He was engaged in animated conversation with a number of respected elders from around the region. She could not penetrate their squabbling. She only caught bits and pieces. There were cries about the prophets and repeated shouts about the Law. But she was not concerned about such endless disputes men were forever engaged in. Her daughter lay sick unto death at home, and as far as she was concerned, the Law and a thousand prophets could very well wait. Let them ask her, and she would tell them what really mattered. Life is what matters. My daughter's life. What good is any Law to someone who is dead? Restore my daughter, and then you can squabble all you want about what you think the Law wants from her.

"Sir!" she cried, all the louder, nudging her way through the crowd to get closer. The others were annoyed at her insistence and showed it by glaring at her. He, however, caught her in the side of his eyes but carried on unabated.

She continued to fight her way into their midst. "Please, sir. Please, I beg of you," she cried. Some of the spectators at the fringe of the group blocked her progress by forcibly holding her back. Even the disputants were distracted by her antics. Still, he paid her no mind whatsoever and drew them back into the discussion. That should be answer enough for her, they thought. Well, they thought wrong. It might have been enough if it was for herself that she was pleading. But it was not near enough to deter her from fighting for her daughter's life. She would hound heaven and hell itself if she had to.

She was causing such a commotion it was embarrassing. Even his disciples were rather surprised at Jesus' apparent disregard of her. Well, if he wasn't inclined to do anything for her, then he should tell her and get rid of her before she ruined the favorable impression he was making on the local townspeople. Of course, it was Peter who spoke up.

"Do something about her. She's spoiling everything." Before he could say another word, the woman realizing that the crowd would let her advance no further, cried out at the top of her voice, "Please sir, I beg of you. Please come. My daughter is dying."

Jesus continued to ignore her. John told him, "This

woman dogs after you to the point of distraction. If you are not of a mind to help her, you had best send her away, otherwise all will be lost, and we might as well leave."

John was taken aback by the harshness of Jesus' reply. Just as defiantly as the woman, he shouted for all in the crowd to hear. "I have come for the sake of the family of Israel. It is not right that I should give the food of children to dogs!"

The crowd was dumbstruck at his outburst. Peter was immediately deflated. He knew what it meant to be hot-headed and to put your foot into it, but this loss of control just when Jesus had the crowd eating out of his hand was completely inexplicable. John was appalled. The others were simply aghast.

Well, the crowd may have been struck dumb, but not her. She came back at him without batting an eye. It was as if the crowd had been hushed just so that she could be heard.

"You are right!" she cried. "But even the dogs are allowed to eat the crumbs that fall from the family table."

For the first time, Jesus looked directly at the woman. A barely perceptible smile creased his lips. "Woman, go home. Your daughter is healed." Having said that, he turned back to the others and resumed where they left off.

It was like a stone that is tossed into a pond. It made its splash, and then the waters surged back, and everything returned to normal.

The discussion continued for some time longer and finally ended. The crowd broke up, but Jesus and his disciples remained until the very last straggler departed. As they made to leave, the woman alone remained standing there in their path.

Jesus said to her. "I told you that your daughter was healed. Did you not believe me?"

"Yes, Master. I believe just as you told me that when I go home my daughter will be healed."

"Then why have you not gone home?"

"Because I have a son at home, too."

"Is he also sick?"

"No, Master."

"Then what more do you want?"

"Sir. Can I go home with a gift for my daughter and nothing for my son?"

A flood of warmth flushed his face. "What is it you want for him?" he asked.

"A blessing," she replied.

Jesus turned to his disciples and said, "The heart of God is a mother's love."

———

Everything that happens to us in life becomes a filter through which the grace of God must pass in order to reach our hearts and then pass through again in order to reach that of our neighbor.

———

Prayers are not plea bargains. They are acts of adoration.

ANGELFLAKES

*B*ethlehem, Montana, like its namesake in Israel, is a little town. It is comfortably nestled in the foothills of the Rocky Mountains between Great Falls and Helena and rates no more attention than as a brief rest stop for excited tourists hurrying to see the panoramic view from Scapegoat Mountain in the summer and tired skiers returning home to the big city in the winter. It boasts a population of 515 and growing, but not much faster than a tortoise in a race with the hares around it. The business district, if you can call it that, consists of the Buck's

Trading Post and General Store—a name indicative of the town's unwillingness to part with the past—Aunt Bea's Mountain Cookery, Fred's Gas Station, and the Bethlehem Church. It once had a more formal sounding church name, but everyone called it "the church" for so long that when Bart Simms painted the sign he just wrote Bethlehem Church and gave it a new christening.

It was at the church hall where all the townspeople were gathering on Christmas Eve for their customary pot luck supper and worship service. Along with the sunrise service at Easter, everyone "without exception" was there, except old Tom Billings who gave up on church long ago when his dreams of making it big prospecting for gold died along with his wife in the fall of 1954. He wasn't mean or ornery about it as one might expect. It's just that he had always been a quiet man and he simply became a recluse after that. Everything the people of Bethlehem did, they did together "without exception—except for old Tom Billings."

This Christmas the holiday spirit was woefully lacking. That, too, was without exception considering no one knew how Tom Billings was feeling on this cold, gloomy, and dismal evening. The church's still-new carillon was playing the customary Christmas carols, which should have brightened everybody's spirits the way they did last year, but the songs got lost in the howling wind sweeping down from Canada. The hall was decorated with fresh pine boughs that spread their sweet fragrance over the gathering, but no one took notice. Even as they ate there were no boisterous outbreaks of hearty laughter or children's shouts. Families spoke barely above a whisper. Even the children acted subdued although they hardly knew why. It was just that they could sense the somber atmosphere, like being at a wake or the bedside of a sick person, so they reacted accordingly. It was Christmas Eve and something was wrong.

When the meal was finished, the women gathered in the kitchen to wash the dishes while the men took down the tables and prepared the hall for the gathering after worship when there would be an exchange of gifts. The children, of course, were restless.

"What are we going to do?" Lucy asked her mother. Ordinarily, the kids would all scoot outside at this time to play in the snow, only this year there was none. Instead, it was raining, and what little snow remained from the last snowfall had melted into mud. Consequently, they were bored and restless.

"Why don't you and your brother and the others ask the pastor to tell you a story while we're getting things ready for after church."

Finding nothing better to do, the children decided to follow her advice and seek him out. It's not that they minded listening to his stories, for he was truly a wonderful storyteller; it's just that kids would rather play than listen.

They found him in his study going over his notes for his Christmas sermon. He looked up at the children pouring into the room. "What's this?" he asked, as they circled his big oak desk.

"We can't go outside to play because it's raining," Lucy said.

"So Mom said we should ask you to tell us a story," Twig, her younger brother, interrupted her before she could finish. No one remembered his real name any more. He got dubbed Twig by his father, who said that because he got into so much trouble for a little guy he was going to be the last twig on the family tree. Lucy hated it when he interrupted her, so she gave him "that older sister look." But he opened the floodgate and a whole torrent of questions poured forth from the children. They all wanted to know why everybody and everything was so gloomy this Christmas.

"I see," the old pastor said. "So you've noticed it, too."

The children all nodded their heads, proud at being so observant.

"What's the matter?" Twig asked and got the look again.

"Before I answer that, Twig, let me ask you children a question. Have you all been feeling glum and moody lately?"

"Yes," they replied and nodded their heads.

"Why is that?"

"Because it's been raining and gloomy for days and days," Lucy answered before Twig could say anything. Nonetheless, he followed it up immediately with, "And there's no snow!"

Once Twig mentioned the absence of snow all the other children chimed their agreement, so he stuck his tongue out at Lucy. She would have throttled him right then and there, but the pastor interrupted. "That's it! That's it exactly," he exclaimed. "But it's not the absence of snowflakes that everyone misses this Christmas, but angelflakes."

The children stood there dumbfounded over what he said. From the looks on their faces no one had ever heard anything even remotely like it.

"What's angelflakes?" Twig asked.

"Well, now," the old man said settling comfortably in his chair. "Snowflakes are what you get during the winter. Angelflakes are what you get on Christmas Eve."

From past experience the children knew that he was about to tell them a story so they settled down right where they were. "I still don't know what they are," Twig said before his sister grabbed him and plopped him down on the floor.

* * *

"A long, long time ago God told the angels in heaven that he just had a wonderful idea. He was going to create a whole universe of stars. Millions and billions of them.

"'What for?' the angel Gabriel asked." The pastor smiled at Twig who was just about to interrupt him to ask the same question.

"'Just for something to do,' God said. So God made the entire universe and everything that's in it.

"'Now what?' Gabriel asked because he found this rather boring.

"'I suppose I could create life,' God said. 'That might liven things up and make it more exciting.' So God made all kinds of living things—all kinds of plants and all kinds of animals."

"I know," Twig interrupted. "And people too."

"Shut up, Twig!" Lucy said, grabbing his shoulder and shaking it.

The pastor continued with his story.

"'That's better.' Gabriel said, looking at what God had done. 'But not much.'

"'Well, how about if I were to make people?' God asked.

"'Now you're talking,' Gabriel said. 'Then we angels would have friends we could talk to and play with.' So God made Adam and Eve and a whole host of people. It was wonderful, at first. Angels and people got along really well together. They talked together, worked together, and played together."

"You mean they could actually see angels and talk to them?" Naturally, it was Twig who voiced the question all the children were wondering about. He simply beat everybody else to it, as usual.

"Just like the way we do with each other," the pastor said.

"Then how come we don't see them anymore?"

Lucy could stand it no longer. She punched her brother in the back and warned him to shut up. Twig was about to retaliate when the pastor interrupted them by saying, "Because the people did a bad thing. They sinned."

Twig and Lucy felt guilty so they stopped scuffling.

"The angels had never seen people do anything bad before. Sin upset them a great deal. They wanted to get as far away from it as possible so they went to heaven. From up there they could watch what was going on with people.

"Then, when Cain killed his brother Abel, the angels up in heaven began to cry. Sin was not just a bad thing, it was a sad thing. And the worse people got, the more the angels cried. Lots and lots of tears because there are lots and lots of angels. Nevertheless, people just seemed to keep on sinning. They were lying, cheating, stealing, swearing, hurting, and killing. Heaven got filled to overflowing with tears until it could hold them back no longer. The gates of heaven opened like a floodgate, and a torrential downpour fell upon the earth. There were so many tears up there that it rained for forty days and forty nights until the entire earth was covered with water. Only one man and his family managed to save themselves from the great flood."

"Noah!" Lucy shouted before Twig could say anything. He wouldn't have said anything anyways because he hadn't gotten that far in Bible school.

But, so as not to be outdone by his sister, he did say, "You mean rain is angeltears?"

"Sometimes," the pastor said continuing with his tale. "But, that was such a terrible tragedy God said that He would never allow it to happen again.

"'Well then, tell your people to stop sinning,' Gabriel said to God. 'I can't help it if they make my angels cry.'

"So God sent prophets to tell the people when the flood-waters were getting dangerously high in heaven and sometimes they listened. But, then, only for a while. It seemed that people just got used to sinning against one another. So the more they sinned, the more the angels cried. After a while heaven was getting as filled up as it was in the days of Noah.

"'You'd better do something and fast,' Gabriel told God. 'Whether You like it or not this could bring about an even worse flood.'

"'You know, I've grown real attached to people,' God said wistfully. 'When they're good, they're very good, and they please me ever so much.'

"'And when they're bad, they're really bad,' Gabriel sighed. 'I tell you, the floodgates are bursting at the seams and I don't know how much longer we can hold them back. It's going to take something drastic to stop this flood.'

"'I know!' God exclaimed. 'Maybe if I gave them something better than anything I've ever given them before, better than anything in the whole world, even better than anything in the whole universe, something so wonderful it will take their minds off everything else, and they will never sin again.'"

"What's that?" Twig asked.

"'What if I gave them a son! My son,'" the pastor answered without breaking stride.

"'Yes!' Gabriel shouted. 'That'll do it. It's a great idea. That should make them stop sinning and bring peace to the earth once again.'

"So the plans were made and Gabriel told Mary of Nazareth what God was going to do and she agreed. So, she and Joseph traveled to Bethlehem where the great event was to take place.

"Meanwhile all the angels of heaven looked down on what was happening, and their hearts were filled with joy and anticipation. The shepherds gathered to hear the good news, and the Magi set out on their long journey. Everything was proceeding according to plan.

"But sin is very strong, and it doesn't give up easily. In Jerusalem, the wicked King Herod learned about the birth of the new king and was filled with jealousy and hate. He was not going to have another king come along and try to take his place. He would do everything in his power to stop this child. He didn't care what it took, even if he had to kill every baby in Bethlehem, he was going to do it.

"When the angels in heaven heard what King Herod planned, there was no holding back their tears. They started to cry uncontrollably. Millions of angels began crying billions of tears. Gabriel became frantic. He pleaded with them to stop otherwise the world would be flooded again—and much, much worse than before.

"But, it was useless. What Herod wanted to do was more terrible than anything they could have ever imagined. They couldn't stop themselves from crying even if they wanted to."

"But, God said that He wouldn't ever flood the world again," Lucy cried out remembering her catechism.

"I'm afraid there was just no stopping this flood," the old pastor continued. "The floodgates burst open once again and a torrent greater than the one of Noah's time began to fall toward earth.

"'I tried,' Gabriel sighed.

"'I know,' God said."

At this point the pastor paused in his story. He looked to see if the sadness of sin was impacting on the children. It was there, unmistakably. Even Twig could think of nothing to say. He continued.

"Now at this point in the story, children, you must understand that two big angel teardrops led the way down. The one teardrop said to the other, 'It's really too bad that the earth is going to be flooded again.'

"'I suppose it's unavoidable seeing that people won't stop sinning,' the other teardrop answered. 'Everywhere you look they're still lying, cheating, stealing, and fighting. This flood will never stop until all the people are all gone. Even God can't stop this now.'"

"I'll bet he can if he wanted to!" Twig shouted, startling everyone.

"'Look!'" the pastor shouted before the spell was broken. He pointed downward as if he were one of the teardrops. "Look! Look down there.

"'Where?' the other teardrop asked.

"'Down there at Bethlehem.'

"The two teardrops strained real hard until they could see below them a stable where some shepherds were gathering.

"'What are they doing?" the first teardrop asked.

"'It looks like they're bringing gifts.' The second teardrop strained even harder to make out what was happening. 'Yes, that's it! They're bringing gifts to God's son.'

"'I can see it,' the first one shouted excitedly. 'That's what they're doing. They're bringing gifts to the baby Jesus. In the midst of all this terrible sadness. Why it's so beautiful, it's enough to give you the chills.'

"And that's exactly what it did, children," the old pastor said. "It gave them the chills."

"'Look over there,'" the first teardrop shouted again pointing to the entrance of the stable. Three Wise Men entered also bearing gifts. 'Wow! Look at that! They're bringing gold, frankincense, and myrrh. What great gifts. It's enough to give you the shivers.'

"And that's just what it did, children. It gave them the shivers."

"As the two teardrops drew closer and closer to the earth, they could see more and more. There were people all over the earth bringing gifts. God made it so that they could suddenly see far into the future where thousands and thousands of people were gathering at Christmas to bring thousands and thousands of gifts and wish peace to one another in honor of his son.

"'Golly! It's enough to give you the goose bumps,' they said together.

"And you know children, that's exactly what it did. It gave them goose bumps. Big, funny shaped goose bumps that stuck out all over their bodies. Along with the chills and the shivers, too.

"And that's when they noticed it," he said pointing up to the sky. "They suddenly realized that weren't speeding toward earth any more. They had slowed down. As a matter of fact they were floating down, slowly and gently.

"'Hey. Look at us!' they shouted. 'We're all white and pretty.'

"'So are we!' shouted all the other angel teardrops who were watching and listening to everything they said. When they looked at one another, they saw that they all had turned into big, white, beautiful snowflakes. Or, I should say . . . angelflakes. You see, angelflakes are angel tears that get the goosebumps when people do something nice.

"So God kept his word and the earth wasn't flooded. Instead, it was blanketed with a pretty, white snowfall on that very first Christmas Eve.

"'I knew you could do it,' Gabriel said to God."

"So did I," said Twig.

However, the story was not quite over yet. It needed a moral, so the pastor continued.

"'But, *I* didn't do it,' God responded. 'The people did it. When they act kind or good or loving, they can change teardrops into snowflakes.'"

"Angel tears into angelflakes," Lucy chimed in.

"That's right," the pastor agreed, pleased that the children were getting the meaning of his story. "That's why everyone's so gloomy this Christmas. There's no snow, and we've all been hoping for a white Christmas."

"Maybe, if we did a lot of nice things for each other we can still change those angel tears outside into angelflakes," Twig suggested.

"Who knows? It just might work, Twig. But, now it's time for our church service. I can hear the bell ringing."

* * *

After the service, when the people gathered in the hall once again for the exchange of gifts, it was still drizzling outside. But everyone seemed a little bit happier now than before, and the children were being especially good.

When the festivities ended and they all went outside to make for home, there still was no snow. Then, just as Lucy stepped off the last step leading down from the church, she slipped and fell into a puddle of mud. Everyone including the pastor expected Twig to be the first one to burst out laughing at his sister's misfortune. Instead, he surprised the entire congregation by hurrying over to help her.

"Did you see that, Frank?" his mother said to her husband. She was in a state of shock.

"I see it, but I don't believe it," he answered. "It must be Christmas."

Twig helped his sister up and began to clean her off.

"Twig," his mother shouted. "You're actually giving me the goose bumps."

When the children heard this, they all burst into laughter. The adults looked at them, bewildered. Then, a big, beautiful, lumbering snowflake landed on Twig's nose. It took them all by surprise. When they looked up the heavens were filled with a gently falling snow.

One of the adults shouted, "Look kids! Snowflakes."

"No," the kids answered in chorus. "They're angelflakes."

To ask man to talk about God is like asking the night to describe the rainbow.

🌿